The

HERITAGE
BOOK

1 9 9 7

The
HERITAGE
BOOK
1997

Edna McCann

Prentice Hall Canada Inc.
Scarborough, Ontario

ISBN 0-13-263070-2

1 2 3 4 5 01 00 99 98 97

Printed and bound in Canada

Acquisitions Editor: Sara Borins	Art Director: Kyle Gell
Production Editor: Kelly Dickson	Cover Design: Julia Hall
Copy Editor: Ann McInnis	Interior Design: Olena Serbyn
Production Coordinator: Julie Preston	Page Layout: Joan Morrison

This book is set in 12/13 1/2 New Caledonia.

Literary Credits:

Page 11 The Literary Trustees of Walter de la Mare, and The Society of Authors as their representative.

Page 24 "Wouldn't Take Nothing For My Journey Now," Maya Angelou, © 1993, Random House Inc.

Page 31 "Good Hours" from The Poetry of Robert Frost, Robert Frost, © Henry Holt and Company, Inc.

Pages 62 and 104 used with the permission of The Helen Steiner Rice Foundation, Cincinnati, Ohio, ©1976 The Helen Steiner Rice Foundation, All Rights Reserved.

Page 154 "The Corner of the Year." Reprinted with the permission of Simon & Schuster from The Collected Poems of Robert P. Tristram Coffin. Copyright © 1948 by Robert P. Tristram Coffin, Renewed 1976.

Photo Credits

Winter	Spring	Summer	Autumn
Gord Handley	Florence Gillespie	Gord Handley	Gord Handley
Gord Handley	Gord Handley	Kathleen Bellesiles	Gord Handley
Charlene Daley	Charlene Daley	Florence Gillespie	Gord Handley
Gord Handley	Charlene Daley	Gord Handley	Florence Gillespie
Charlene Daley	Florence Gillespie	Charlene Daley	Gord Handley
Gord Handley	Vince Farr	AngelaWheelock	Gord Handley
AngelaWheelock	Angela Wheelock	Florence Gillespie	Angela Wheelock
Gord Handley	Charlene Daley	AngelaWheelock	Vince Farr

Introduction

Putting together the *Heritage Books* has been one of the great joys of my life for over twenty years, and this volume continues the tradition. Yes, with each new year, I look back on fond memories—but I also look with optimism to the future. For I believe that life just keeps getting better. And it is this belief that I want to share with my readers.

I see the passage of time in terms of gains. A new friend. A new grandchild. New experiences and challenges. Each new day has the promise of creating a special memory: walking in new-fallen snow; watching the sun set; meeting a dear friend for tea; or reading a story to a child.

Given the choice, I would not want to be twenty again. Indeed, all of our life experiences make us what we are and help us to grow and blossom!

I hope that you all take pleasure in the 1997 edition of the *Heritage Book*. May these stories, quotations, poems, and anecdotes bring you as much joy and cheer as they have brought me.

Edna McCann

January

Wednesday January 1

THE year is gone! The year is gone!
I heard your sad sweet carillon:
A year of gladness, and of fears,
A year of laughter, and of tears,
A time of sun, a time of shower
A time of frost, a time of flower…
Though I might fare to other climes,
Nor hear your silver-throated chimes
Yet would my heart be glad—would sing
For hours you gave…remembering.
Another year! Another year!
I hear your voice ring, loud and clear,
While singing, flinging from your tower,
Those singing notes that mark the hour.
And faithfully, as other times
Hope rings the tenor of your chimes;
Another birth—another spring!
New courage; bright new hope you bring
A better day; a brighter dawn!
Sweet bells ring on! Ring on!

With these words penned by Blanche DeGood
Lofton I wish you the happiest of New Years.

Thursday January 2

WHERE does the time go?
I must ask this question every year at this time but it is hard to imagine that another twelve months have gone by so quickly.

Last night we reviewed our calendar for 1996. This has become a tradition for us over the past few years and it really is a wonderful way to remember what has transpired in those days that have passed.

"The twins' birthday," "Marg and Bruce's anniversary," "Strawberry Social," "visit from Ben and Marie" bring laughter and joy as we share the happy memories of these occasions.

Sometimes we share tears as well, as with "Betty's funeral" and the loss of a dear and faithful friend.

The memo calendar really is a diary of our day-to-day life and an interesting and enjoyable "book" to read as we begin another new year.

Friday January 3

CHANGE is the law of life. And those who look away only to the past or the present are certain to miss the future.

John F. Kennedy

Saturday January 4

TODAY was a "catch up" day in our home. We needed to catch up on our cleaning, catch up on some reading of Christmas letters that received only a quick glance as they arrived over the holidays, and we needed to catch up on some much-missed quiet time.

One of the great joys of a large family is that holidays are never a lonely time, with some or all members getting together to share in the festivities.

When you are as old as I am, however, these long hectic days can become almost a burden unless you are able to find some place to spend some restful time alone.

I am fortunate to have my own "apartment" in my daughter's home and I will often retreat to the quiet of my bedroom knowing that I will be undisturbed as I rejuvenate myself.

Even so it comes as somewhat of a relief when we say goodbye to our loved ones and life returns to a slower pace that "old folks" like me enjoy.

Sunday January 5

AND on the seventh day God ended his work which he had made; and he rested on the seventh day....

Genesis 2:2

Monday January 6

Today is Epiphany, the day that we commemorate the coming of the Three Wise Men, who were led by the Star of Bethlehem to the infant Jesus.

"And, lo, the star, which they saw in the east, went before them, till it came and stood over where the young child was. When they saw the star, they rejoiced with exceeding great joy. And when they were come into the house, they saw the young child with Mary his mother, and fell down, and worshipped him: and when they had opened their treasures, they presented unto him gifts; gold, and frankincense, and myrrh."

Matthew 2:9-11

Tuesday January 7

If you were going to die soon and had only one phone call you could make, who would you call and what would you say? And why are you waiting?

Stephen Levine

Wednesday January 8

I KNOW of no more encouraging fact than the un-questionable ability of man to elevate his life by conscious endeavour.

Henry David Thoreau

Thursday January 9

LIVE not in yesterdays,
Look back and you may sorrow.
Live precisely for today,
Look forward to tomorrow.

J.J. Hulsgen

Friday January 10

O N these cold January days I look forward to my daily walk.

No, I don't need to bundle myself up in layers of clothing with boots and gloves and a hat. I am ready to walk with only warm slacks and a sweater and a good pair of walking shoes.

The secret to this daily regimen is that I am a "mall walker." Each morning in shopping malls across the country many senior citizens (and others) arrive before the opening of the stores to walk up and down the "traffic-free" interior corridors.

Our walking group usually starts at about 8:30 a.m. and each person sets his or her own pace according to health and ability.

Recently our mall owner has added "walking music," a varied selection of songs designed to add interest to our strolls.

You might want to join the group in your area.

Saturday January 11

MY friend Jake Frampton came in to visit today. My former readers will remember that Jake owns a bookstore and has been kind enough to encourage my love of reading by bringing me many books, both old and new, to enjoy.

Although I take pleasure in reading all types of books I confess that mysteries or books that are humorous are my real favourites.

Jake brought me a book today that has been around for a number of years and was on the New York Times bestseller list for many months. *Chicken Soup for the Soul* was written and compiled by Jack Canfield and Mark Victor Hansen.

These are two of America's best-loved inspirational speakers and between them they have come up with the very best of their collected stories that have touched the hearts of people everywhere.

Jack Canfield is the president of Self Esteem Seminars and he has conducted personal and professional development seminars worldwide.

Mark Victor Hansen is a motivator who travels 250,000 miles a year to present his powerful message of encouragement.

Together they have given us an inspirational book that I am very much looking forward to reading.

Sunday January 12

LET the words of my mouth, and the meditation of my heart, be acceptable in thy sight, O Lord, my strength, and my redeemer.

Psalm 19:14

Monday January 13

OUR moments of inspiration are not lost though we have no particular poem to show for them; for those experiences have left an indelible impression, and we are ever and anon reminded of them.

Henry David Thoreau

Tuesday January 14

O N February 3, 1943, the transport "Dorchester" was torpedoed off the coast of Greenland. As the ship was sinking, four chaplains—one a Catholic, one a Jew, and two Protestants—were on deck passing out life belts. When there were none left, they gave their own away. As the ship went down the four chaplains stood arm in arm, praying.

This is what religion is all about.

Wednesday January 15

I s there anything nicer on a cold winter's night than a steaming bowl of homemade soup?

Hearty rotini chicken soup is delicious and easy to make. Add crusty rolls and some cheddar cheese and you have a tasty winter meal guaranteed to chase those January chills.

5 cups chicken broth
3 carrots, sliced
2 cups broccoli florets
1 cup fresh mushrooms
1 cup sliced celery
1 onion, chopped
3 cloves garlic, minced
1/4 of a 500-gram package of rotini
2 cups cubed cooked chicken
salt & pepper to taste

Bring the broth to a boil in a large saucepan. Add the carrots, broccoli, mushrooms, celery, onions and garlic. Simmer, covered, for 15 minutes. Cook the rotini according to package directions. Stir rotini and chicken into the soup; heat through. Makes 10 servings.

Thursday January 16

ALL of us could take a lesson from the weather. It pays no attention to criticism.

Friday January 17

EARLIER this week our American friends celebrated the birthday of Reverend Martin Luther King, Jr.

Dr. King was the inspirational leader of the civil rights movement in the turbulent 1960s.

"Pity may represent little more than the impersonal concern which prompts the mailing of a cheque, but true sympathy is the personal concern which demands the giving of one's soul."

Martin Luther King, Jr.

Saturday January 18

THERE is very little on television that I enjoy watching more than the figure skating presentations that are so popular at this time of year. The skills demonstrated by these young men and women are of such a high level that at times it is difficult to comprehend what the eyes are seeing. Triple jumps, quadruple jumps, and flips are a regular part of each skater's routine as are the footwork patterns and the intricate choreography that pull the routines together.

At times these presentations are nearly heart-stopping to see—however, I watch bravely on and love every minute of it.

Sunday January 19

REST of the weary,
Joy of the sad,
Hope of the dreary,
Light of the glad,
Home of the stranger,
Strength to the end,
Refuge from danger,
Saviour and Friend.

Rev. J.S.B. Monsell
The Book of Common Praise

Monday January 20

SMILE at each other, smile at your wife, smile at your husband, smile at your children, smile at each other—it doesn't matter who it is—and that will help you to grow up in greater love for each other.

Mother Teresa

Tuesday January 21

To know how to grow old is the master work of wisdom, and one of the most difficult chapters in the great art of living.

Wednesday January 22

I ENJOY the poetry of Walter de la Mare and I offer his lines on "The Snowflake" for you today.

See, now, this filigree: 'tis snow,
Shaped, in the void, of heavenly dew;
On winds of space like flower to blow
In the wilderness of blue.
Black are those pines. The utter cold
Hath frozen to silence the birds' green woods.
Rime hath ensteeled the wormless mould
A vacant quiet broods.
Lo, this entrancèd thing!—a breath
Of life that bids Man's heart to crave
Still for perfection: ere fall death,
And earth shut in his grave.

Thursday January 23

I HAD no shoes and complained until I met a man who had no feet.

Friday January 24

A NY failure will tell you that success is nothing but luck.

Saturday January 25

M Y daughter Julia is an executive with a large Canadian firm. Her position requires her to spend much of the year in other parts of the world, so, when she called to say that she was home and looking forward to a visit with Marg and me, we were thrilled. You see Marg and I have come to enjoy world travelling vicariously, through Julia. We were not disappointed as she took us through her recent visit to Hawaii.

I have always pictured Hawaii as an island with luxurious hotels and endless beaches. In fact the Hawaiian Islands have 21 of the world's climatic zones ranging from lush tropical rain forests to alpine summits.

The diversity of life that evolved in Hawaii is unique. Ninety percent of the flora exists no place else in the world. Hawaii is much younger than the rest of the world, these volcanic islands forming long after the other lands bore footprints.

There are many parks—a few of which are underwater. These marine-life sanctuaries harbour thousands of reef fish in dazzling colours which draw divers and snorkelers in large numbers.

Hawaii looks like a small paradise. Maybe someday. . . .

Sunday January 26

THEY that wait upon the Lord shall renew their strength; they shall mount up with wings as eagles; they shall run, and not be weary, and they shall walk, and not faint.

Isaiah 40:31

Monday January 27

I THINK that wherever your journey takes you, there are new gods waiting there, with divine patience—and laughter.

Susan M. Watkins

Tuesday January 28

ONE of the finest movies to come out of Hollywood in recent memory was "Forrest

Gump." This film was about a man who, in spite of a limited ability to learn, lived a life that enthralled audiences both young and old.

It was interesting to hear that Tom Hanks, who won the Oscar for best actor in the film's title role, thought that the movie would bomb.

"We didn't know if people would care about this man's life."

He was proved wrong in a very big way.

Wednesday January 29

SEEK ye counsel of the aged for their eyes have looked on the faces of the years and their ears have harkened to the voices of Life. Even if their counsel is displeasing to you, pay heed to them.

Kahlil Gibran

Thursday January 30

I WENT to our local school this morning to participate in the "Grand-Timers" program.

This program has been running in our area for a number of years now and each year membership in the program has increased. "Grand-Timers" are senior citizens who have some time to give as volunteer readers to the youngsters who, for whatever reasons, have not been read to on a regular basis.

Many of these children are not yet able to read well on their own but often, by the end of the school year, have shown considerable progress.

Our local nursing home, with the assistance of the Lions Club wheelchair bus, is now providing many members of our "Grand" club.

Friday January 31

I WAS interested to learn that Charles Schulz, the creator of "Peanuts," had his cartoons rejected by his high school yearbook staff. He took a correspondence course in cartoon drawing, then applied for a cartoonist's job at Walt Disney studios. He was turned down.

Luckily for us who enjoy Charlie Brown and his dog Snoopy, Schulz persevered.

You don't have to be a genius, you don't need enormous talent, you just have to keep plugging away.

February

Saturday February 1

THIS evening I was remembering the wonder-ful Saturday nights that George and the girls and I enjoyed together so long ago. George would always be sure to have his Sunday sermon completed by Friday so that we could spend Saturdays with our daughters, and often their friends as well.

This poem "Winter Fun" by Elva Weber brings back those happy memories.

When the winter evenings lengthen
And the daily chores are done,
Then we gather round the fireside
For a bit of family fun.
Logs of apple wood lie burning
In the fireplace, embers bright,
Heaps of popcorn slowly dribble
From the spider, gleaming white.
Fun and laughter, games and music
Echo through each room and hall;
Winter evening's time for playing—
We left care with passing fall.

Let the moonbeams cast their shadows
On the snow-clad earth tonight,
We will bind our family closer
By the cozy fireplace light.

Sunday February 2

LIGHTEN our darkness, we beseech thee, O Lord; and by thy great mercy defend us from all perils and dangers of the night; for the love of thy only son, our Saviour Jesus Christ.

The Book of Common Prayer

Monday February 3

YESTERDAY was "Groundhog Day" and as has been the case for the past several years our prognosticating furry friend has again predicted six more weeks of winter.

Although Groundhog Day is really just for fun, "Wiarton Willie" has proven to be quite accurate in his forecasts. According to the announcer on the radio yesterday he is running at above 90% correct, which is considerably more accurate than the meteorologists and forecasters who have access to the latest scientific equipment used in weather tracking.

No matter who tells me, I am never too excited to hear of more winter weather to come.

Tuesday February 4

EVERY leaf and twig was this morning covered with a sparkling ice armour; even the grasses in exposed fields were hung with innumerable diamond pendants, which jingled merrily when brushed by the foot of the traveler. It was literally the wreck of jewels and the crash of gems. . . . Such is beauty ever—neither here nor there, now nor then,—neither in Rome nor in Athens, but wherever there is a soul to admire. If I seek her elsewhere because I do not find her at home, my search will prove a fruitless one.

Henry David Thoreau

Wednesday February 5

A MAN is like a fraction whose numerator is what he is and whose denominator is what he thinks of himself. The larger the denominator the smaller the fraction.

Leo Tolstoy

Thursday February 6

NO situation is so bad that losing your temper won't make it worse.

Friday February 7

FOR many years I have read the *Toronto Star* newspaper. To be honest, as the news has become more and more violent I often just read the travel section and the comics before I move on to do the daily crossword puzzle.

However, the real reason that I chose to read the *Toronto Star* was because of one columnist whose writings I enjoyed immensely. That writer was Gary Lautens, who began his career as a crime and sports writer in Hamilton, Ontario and who, before his death in 1992, won two Stephen Leacock Awards for humour—one for *Take My Family...Please!* in 1981 and another for *No Sex Please...We're Married* in 1984.

He married his wife Jackie ("the Resident Love Goddess") in 1957 and their children Stephen, born in 1959, Jane, 1962, and Richard ("The Rotten Kid"), in 1964, along with Jackie, provided anecdotes and humorous stories that kept readers of the *Toronto Star* amused for years.

Lautens used his stories about his family to talk about life and people, which probably explains his wide appeal.

His son Stephen wrote, "Dad wasn't just writing about our family, but about every family. Or sometimes the semi-mythical ideal family we would all like to belong to."

I miss his column more and more.

Saturday February 8

NEVER mistake knowledge for wisdom. One helps you make a living; the other helps you make a life.

Sandra Carey

Sunday February 9

THE righteous shall be glad in the Lord, and shall trust in him; and all the upright in heart shall glory.

Psalm 64:10

Monday February 10

SINCE reading is the basis on which most of our education is built, it is crucial that children develop a love of books and of reading.

One wise mother in our neighbourhood gave her young son a comfortable reading spot of his own. In a corner of his room she placed a beanbag chair, a cozy blanket and a small bookshelf with his favourite books.

He uses his reading corner often and is probably well on his way to becoming a book lover for life.

Tuesday February 11

TOMORROW is the birthday of one of America's greatest presidents, Abraham Lincoln.

Abe Lincoln was an excellent example of persistence.

Born in the poorest of circumstances, he faced defeat throughout his life. He lost eight elections, failed twice in business and suffered a nervous breakdown. Lesser men would have given up many times.

Said Mr. Lincoln, "The sense of obligation to continue is present in all of us. A duty to strive is the duty of us all. I felt a call to that duty."

Wednesday February 12

ASH WEDNESDAY

SPARE thy people, O Lord, and give not thine heritage to reproach, that the heathen should rule over them: wherefore should they say among the people, Where is their God?

Joel 2:17

Thursday February 13

PERHAPS the greatest social service that can be rendered by anybody to the country and to mankind is to bring up a family.

George Bernard Shaw

Friday February 14

VALENTINE'S DAY

Many years have had their passing
Since we told each other, dear,
We would share life's joys and sorrows,
Close together year by year.
We have traveled love's good highway
Over hills and through the dales,
Finding sunshine on the pathway,
Smiling bravely through the gales.
Still we're walking on together,
Partners in the game of life,
Hand in hand and heart to heart, dear,
Friends and lovers, man and wife.
Life could hold no richer blessings
As the years pass swiftly by,
Than to find us still good comrades,
Sweethearts, partners, you and I.

Saturday February 15

OVER the past several years I have taken a number of computer courses. Although I don't claim great proficiency on these amazing machines I have become "comfortable" with at least some of their many uses.

One of the most interesting uses I have found is that I may now take a "virtual" tour of Canada.

For example, Vancouver is just a point and a click away.

Many of the larger cities have online magazines and through the listings you can find out where to go and where to avoid if you are a real—or virtual—traveller.

Vancouver has a freenet open to anyone on the Internet. Here you can find anything from museum schedules to road closures during avalanche season.

It is possible to travel in cyberspace from one side of Canada to the other. All of our provinces have tourist information sites and it is quite simple to find your way to them on a "browser."

As well, it is possible to become part of an electronic discussion group on your computer. This is a huge advantage if you are thinking of travelling to a place that you've never been to before. Ask someone in Prince Edward Island about the Oyster Festival before you go.

Using a computer to "travel" is as easy as a point and a click.

Sunday February 16

IF you fulfill the royal law according to the Scripture, You shall love your neighbour as yourself, you do well.

James 2:8

Monday February 17

A YOUNG student gave this explanation for not joining in a class discussion: "I think I'll learn more by listening. Anything I would say I already know."

Tuesday February 18

M AYA Angelou in her book *Wouldn't Take Nothing for My Journey Now* writes:

Since time is the one immaterial object which we cannot influence—neither speed up nor slow down, add to nor diminish—it is an imponderably valuable gift. Each of us has a few minutes a day or a few hours a week which we could donate to an old folks' home or a children's hospital ward. The elderly whose pillows we plump or whose water pitchers we refill may or may not thank us for our gift, but the gift is upholding the foundation of the universe.

Wednesday February 19

A BOUT a year ago a dear friend of mine lost a grandson in a tragic accident. This is probably the worst pain that a parent or grandparent can experience. That part of you that was going to live on after your own death is gone. The question most often asked is "Why them…why not me instead?"

Marg says that although the acute overwhelming pain immediately after his death has faded she has found that it has been replaced with a profound sadness and a deepening depression.

Recognizing that she needs help, she has joined a bereavement support group.

As she explained to me, "I know that the support group cannot bring my grandson back to me or even ease the pain or lessen the sadness but there is some comfort in realizing that there are others experiencing the very same feelings.

"We all suffer the dreadful sorrow of missing our loved ones, and we all seem to have great difficulty sleeping.

"Although it hurts we need to talk about our lost ones. We need to keep them vivid in our minds, afraid that our memories will dim.

"While others may have grown tired of listening, our support group hasn't. Somehow that helps."

Thursday February 20

EACH friend represents a world in us, a world possibly not born until they arrive, and it is only by this meeting that a new world is born.

Anaïs Nin

Friday February 21

IT is important for children to feel confident and secure but sometimes praising them can have the opposite effect.

General praise such as "You're wonderful" may seem to be encouraging but according to experts it is much less effective than describing why they are wonderful in specifics.

For example, instead of saying "What a good girl!" try "I see you got yourself all dressed for school and you've even made your bed. Wow!"

"You did such a good job researching and organizing your project on whales" makes a much greater impression on a child than "You're so smart!"

"You're very kind" won't tell a child nearly as much as "Thanks for sharing your chocolate bar with Kyle. I know that he felt badly because he didn't have one."

Being specific allows children to feel proud of their strengths and abilities rather than being dependent on the approval of others.

Saturday February 22

TODAY is my sister Sarah and her husband Richard's anniversary. As Sarah remarked, "You know, Edna, whenever I think I want to change Richard in some way all I have to do is read these words. They are on the tomb of an Anglican minister buried in the crypts of Westminster Abbey."

—When I was young and free my imagination had no limits, I dreamed of changing the world. As I grew older and wiser, I discovered the world would not change, so I shortened my sights somewhat and decided to change only my country.

But it, too, seemed unmovable.

As I grew into my twilight years, in one last desperate attempt, I settled for changing only my family, those closest to me, but alas, they would have not of it.

And now as I lie on my deathbed, I suddenly realize: "If only I had changed myself first," then by example I would have changed my family.

From their inspiration and encouragement, I would then have been able to better my country and, who knows, I may even haved changed the world.—

"That is all I need to remind me how silly I am."

Sunday February 23

FOR His great love has compassed
Our Nature, and our need
We know not; but He knoweth,
And He will bless indeed.

Therefore, O heavenly Father,
Give what is best to me;
And take the wants unanswered,
As offerings made to Thee.

Anonymous

Monday February 24

M Y good friends Will and Muriel stopped in today with some exciting news. They are going to become great-grandparents for the first time.

Muriel, who is extremely creative, has come up with a wonderful idea for a gift to welcome this new wee family member.

"When my granddaughter Nancy was younger she loved to draw. I saved all of her artwork in a trunk in our basement.

"I am going to reproduce some of my favourite pieces on fabric and then use them to make a quilt for the baby's crib."

I can't think of any gift that will be more cherished.

Tuesday February 25

A T this time of year many people travel south to escape the long northern winter. Some people want the warm weather but aren't keen to drive all the way to Florida. A good friend of Jake's has his own method of determining how far south is far enough.

"You get in your car and start driving," he says. "Each time you stop at a service station you ask if they have anti-freeze. When they ask 'What's anti-freeze?' you know that you've gone far enough."

Wednesday February 26

To affect the quality of the day, that is the highest of the arts.

Henry David Thoreau

Thursday February 27

THERE are certain immutable laws of family life. For instance, when you're all dressed up to go out for a night on the town—the very first child to kiss you goodbye will be the one who's been fingerpainting.

Friday February 28

As my former readers know I have a dear friend Emily, who hails from Philadelphia, but who winters in Florida.

I received a letter from her today from her southern home and imagine my surprise when I found a plane ticket bearing my name on a flight destined for Tampa, Florida.

"Edna, you simply must come!" she wrote. "What on earth is the use of my having a lot of money if I don't use it to enjoy things with my friends. We shall have such fun! Please say you'll come."

How could I refuse such a wonderful invitation?

My ticket is dated March 8th so I have a week to get myself organized.

I must confess that I am as excited as a teenager and looking forward immensely to some "fun in the sun."

March

Saturday March 1

I HAD for my winter evening walk—
No one at all with whom to talk,
But I had the cottages in a row
Up to their shining eyes in snow.
And I thought I had the folk within:
I had the sound of a violin;
I had a glimpse through curtain laces
Of youthful forms and youthful faces.
I had such company outward bound.
I went till there were no cottages found.
I turned and repented, but coming back
I saw no window but that was black.
Over the snow my creaking feet
Disturbed the slumbering village street
Like profanation, by your leave,
At ten o'clock of a winter eve.

Robert Frost

Sunday March 2

BE perfect, be of good comfort, be of one mind, live in peace; and the God of love and peace shall be with you.

II Corinthians 13:11

Monday March 3

I AM very much looking forward to my trip to Florida. The most difficult thing is to decide what to take with me. It has taken a great many years but I have at last realized that travelling "light" is the best way to travel—in other words, the less I have to take the better off I will be.

Marg has offered me her lightweight luggage for which I am very grateful. My bags are sturdy but I believe the manufacturer designed them to survive a trip over Niagara Falls. Empty, they weigh more than a grown man.

Fortunately my summer clothing is clean and ironed—a farsighted fall chore for which I am now grateful.

I am free to spend the rest of the week in joyful anticipation, and really, isn't that half the fun of any trip?

Tuesday March 4

IT is better to be prepared for an opportunity and not have one than to have an opportunity and not be prepared.

Whitney Young, Jr.

Wednesday March 5

I HAVE enjoyed the luxury of good health my whole life. Although I am quite sure that a large part of this is due to good luck rather than good management there are some things that you can do to help yourself, no matter what your age.

1. Eat right. The keys to a healthful diet are balance, variety and moderation.
2. Stay active. Exercise reduces stress, helps maintain a healthy weight and helps ward off life-threatening conditions including heart disease and cancer.
3. Stop smoking. Smoking plays a major role in heart disease, stroke, emphysema and lung cancer.
4. Get enough sleep. People who sleep six hours or fewer a night have poorer health than those who sleep more.
5. Reduce stress. Stress can hamper your immune system and make you more susceptible to infections.

Thursday March 6

İF you have one true friend you have more than your share.

Thomas Fuller

Friday March 7

OBSTACLES are those frightful things you see when you take your eyes off your goal.

Henry Ford

Saturday March 8

I CAN hardly believe it but here I am en route to Florida.

I am travelling on a 747 and the crew of the flight couldn't be kinder.

Marg arranged for me to pre-board—she was probably concerned that I would trample someone in my haste to get to my seat.

Really, it is a wonderful service for those of us who are elderly or for young families who are carrying babies or toddlers.

Once seated comfortably in our seats and joined by the rest of the passengers, we were ready to go.

This is my first time travelling "first class" and I intend to enjoy every minute of it.

Sunday March 9

THESE things I have spoken unto you that in me you might have peace. In the world you shall have troubles: but be happy; I have overcome the world.

John 16:33

Monday March 10

I AM in Madeira Beach, an area near St. Petersburg, Florida and I don't believe that Emily or I have stopped chattering since I arrived.

The most wonderful thing about old friendships is that no matter how long it's been since you've seen each other the conversation picks up as if there had never been a break.

Catching up on the news of our families is, of course, the first priority and then we move along to mutual friends.

As well as chatting we have eaten some wonderful meals.

Last evening we ate an "Early Bird" dinner at the "Hungry Fisherman Restaurant," a lovely place just north of Emily's home on Gulf Blvd. I had forgotten how much I enjoyed grouper, that delicious fish that is so popular here in Florida.

I am a very lucky person.

Tuesday March 11

IT'S easy to be independent when you've got money. But to be independent when you haven't got a thing—that's the Lord's test.

Mahalia Jackson

Wednesday March 12

OUR grandchildren accept us for ourselves, without rebuke or effort to change us, as no one in our entire lives has ever done, not our parents, siblings, spouses, friends—and hardly ever our own grown children.

Ruth Goode

Thursday March 13

WHEN you run into someone who is disagreeable to others, you may be sure he is uncomfortable with himself; the amount of pain we inflict on others is directly proportional to the amount we feel within us.

Sydney J. Harris

Friday March 14

FLORIDA may be just one state but it has many faces. In fact there are seven regions in the state, all quite different one from the other.

Northwest Florida stretches from the fabled Suwannee River on the east of Pensacola on the west border of the state. Here the rivers are crystal clear and Shell Island just off Panama City boasts seven miles of untouched shoreline.

Northeast Florida from north of Jacksonville to Gainesville and east to St. Augustine pays homage to the past. St. Augustine, founded in 1565, is a treasure for those history buffs looking to see the "roots" of this splendid state.

Central East Florida has the most popular coastline in the state. From Daytona's famous racetrack down to the Kennedy Space Centre at Cocoa Beach are family resorts attracting hundreds of thousands each year. Central West Florida is the winter home of the manatees. Visitors can see these sea cows in the shallow, slow-moving rivers. In the Tampa and St. Petersburg areas are alluring island communities.

Southwest Florida is known for the tons of shells that wash up on the beaches of Sanibel, Marco and dozens of other atolls. Long strips of sand and remote barrier islands have an appeal for many.

Southeast Florida has Fort Lauderdale's sugar-white beachfront and Miami's Biscayne Bay plus the Keys.

It's all here in this magnificent state.

Saturday March 15

THIS evening Emily and I enjoyed a delicious meal at one of Emily's favourite restaurants here in Florida, P.J.'s Oyster Bar, near Indian Rocks.

This is a wonderful, "frivolous" restaurant that boasts of P.J., the large green parrot in a cage, calling loudly to patrons as they enter.

Tables are crammed closely together and rolls of paper towel hang on hangers suspended on string and dangling in mid-air like seagulls over each table. Walls are decorated with one and two dollar bills signed by patrons and stapled wherever there is any space. You could spend your mealtime reading "Mary and Bill, Flagstaff, Arizona 1991" or "Jean, Rosie and Kids, Presque Isle 1993."

Waiters and waitresses, clad in T-shirts and shorts, hurry from table to table dealing out dinners like cards from a deck.

However, P.J.'s popularity depends upon its incredibly delicious (and inexpensive) seafood that is by far the best I've ever tasted.

At Emily's suggestion we shared the "Fisherman's platter," a wonderful assortment of fish, shrimps, clams and scallops.

I have a feeling I shall be waddling home!

Sunday March 16

IN the small church that we attended this morning I enjoyed this hymn by Adelaide Proctor.

My God, I thank Thee, who has made
The earth so bright;
So full of splendour and of joy,
Beauty and light;
So many glorious things are here
Noble and right.

Monday March 17

As we enjoyed this beautiful St. Patrick's Day here in the sunny south I was reminded of these lines from John Locke.

O Ireland isn't it grand you look,
Like a bride in her rich adornin',
And with all the pent-up love in my heart
I bid you top o' the mornin'.

Tuesday March 18

A GENIUS is one who shoots at something no one else can see, and hits it.

Wednesday March 19

EMILY and I went for a long walk along the beach this evening. There is something wonderfully soothing to the soul in a walk where the sand comes up between your toes and the waves roll in endlessly as the sun sinks slowly over the horizon.

Just as the sun set we were witness to one of nature's strange phenomena.

If you watch the sun go down there is a moment just as the sun falls from view when there is a sudden bright green flash. It is quite amazing really—both the colour and the intensity of the flash are dazzling.

It doesn't happen at every sunset but when it does it is a wonder to see.

Later as the stars and the moon began to twinkle and glow over the ocean I marvelled at the vastness of our universe and the beauty of this planet we call earth.

Thursday March 20

WE have no more right to consume happiness without producing it than to consume wealth without producing it.

George Bernard Shaw

Friday March 21

TODAY is the first day of Spring. Here in Florida, with its summer-like weather, the transition from winter to spring is marked only by the increase in the number of tourists as young people flock here to celebrate "Spring Break" from their studies.

For my readers who are looking for some encouraging signs of the new season I offer you excerpts from Margaret Jewell's "It's Spring."

I heard today, therefore I know
It's coming Spring—I heard a crow.
His cawing rang out both loud and clear
As if to say "Take heart, I'm here."
I saw today, it's plain to me
Spring's on its way—what did I see?
Some hardy sparrows on the path
In a melted puddle—taking a bath.
There's a certain feel, it's in the air,
The scent of Spring, how sweet and rare,
You smiled—that's how I really know;
Because my heart tells me it's so.

Saturday March 22

M EN are what their mothers made them.

Ralph Waldo Emerson

Sunday March 23

PALM SUNDAY

I T is good that a man should both hope and quietly wait for the salvation of the Lord.

Lamentations 3:26

Monday March 24

A LARGE number of Emily's friends and neighbours here in Florida are retired couples. Sitting around the pool this morning we got into quite a lively discussion about some of the difficulties that are faced in this new time in a couple's life.

In the traditional families where the wife was the homemaker and the husband the breadwinner there is an enormous adjustment to be made by both partners.

Many of these women have enjoyed years of freedom—children are gone and mates are still working—and they have developed an independent existence where they have volunteered, gone back to school or developed talents.

Their husbands, accustomed to challenge and respect as members of the work force, must redefine their self-image overnight.

It can be a difficult time for both partners.

All agreed that it was important to build up routines, find new goals, and get involved in something that gives a sense of purpose.

Tuesday March 25

I WILL soon be leaving Florida and Emily to return home. How difficult I find it to say goodbye to someone who means so much to me. Others have written of this and I offer some of their thoughts today.

Ever has it been that love knows not its own depth until the hour of separation.

Kahlil Gibran

To leave is to die a little . . . . One leaves behind a little of oneself at any hour, at any place.

Edmond Haracourt

Parting is all we know of heaven and all we need of hell.

Emily Dickinson

Every parting gives a foretaste of death; every coming together again a foretaste of the resurrection.

Arthur Schopenhauer

We only part to meet again.

John Gay

Wednesday March 26

IT is not enough merely to exist. It's not enough to say "I'm earning enough to support my family. I do my work well. I'm a good father, husband, churchgoer."

That's all very well. But you must do something more. Seek always to do some good, somewhere. Every man has to seek in his own way to realize his true worth. You must give some time to your fellow man. Even if it's a little thing, do something for those who need help, something for which you get no pay but the privilege of doing it. For remember, you don't live in a world all your own. Your brothers are here too.

I thank my friend Marcia in Boston who sent me those inspiring words from Albert Schweitzer.

Thursday March 27

THIS could be discouraging news for those of you with young children. It is estimated that the cost of a university education will triple in less than twenty years.

Do you suppose salaries will have tripled too? It's probably best not to count on it.

Friday March 28

IT was a difficult farewell at the airport this morning. Neither Emily nor I wanted our all-too-short visit to end so there we were, two little old ladies blubbering and promising to write soon.

Thankfully the hostess on our flight kept us smiling with amusing stories from other flights. The story I'm about to tell will appeal to my friend Jake, an avid fisherman.

As is the case with any flight that travels over water the hostess explains the use of the emergency life-saving equipment.

"Are there any questions?" she asked when she had finished.

A gentleman's hand shot up. "May we fish from the life rafts?"

The planeload of passengers broke up laughing.

Saturday March 29

LIKE souls that balance joy and rain
With tears and smiles from heaven again
The maiden Spring upon the plain
Came in a sunlit fall of rain.

Sunday March 30

FOR God so loved the world that he gave his only begotten Son, that whosoever believeth in him should not perish, but have everlasting life.

John 3:16

Happy Easter to all.

Monday March 31

EVEN when one has enjoyed a holiday as much as I did, it is a great pleasure to come home. There is a comfort in knowing that the ones we love are nearby and that our own home, however humble, awaits our loving touch.

"Be it ever so humble
There's no place like home."

John Howard Payne

April

Tuesday April 1

APRIL, April,
Laugh thy girlish laughter;
Then, the moment after,
Weep thy girlish tears!
April, that mine ears
Like a lover greetest,
If I tell thee, sweetest,
All my hopes and fears,
April, April,
Laugh thy golden laughter,
But, the moment after,
Weep thy golden tears!

With these lines from William Watson we welcome the beautiful month of April. I must confess that this is a month that is a favourite of mine. Gone are the "brown" days of spring and now we see the return of the green grass. Buds are coming out of the trees and the spring flowers poke their heads up to the warming sun.

April! A time to enjoy.

Wednesday April 2

IN many families today both mother and father work outside the home. It can be very difficult to keep the house running efficiently and happily when everyone comes home tired after a long day at work or school.

Some good friends who are in this position have offered tips that sound very worthwhile. Here are just a few of them.

Mary McConnell says, "No matter how tired we are at night we all choose our outfits to wear on the next day. We lay out everything—underwear, socks, clothes, so that when morning comes we need just get dressed. We aren't looking for missing buttons or clean socks. It's a real morning time-saver."

Jamie, my granddaughter-in-law, says, "Grocery shopping or running errands can be difficult with small children in tow, so my neighbour and I trade baby-sitting services twice a week. It gives each of us a chance to get out alone and it gives our children some time to socialize and play together."

Other hints I've heard include

—keep an event calendar posted for all to see.

—grocery shop in the late evenings when the stores are less crowded.

—give everyone his or her own laundry basket so that, as laundry is being folded, it can be placed in the correct basket.

In these busy times every minute counts.

Thursday April 3

FOR a long time it seemed to me that real life was about to begin, but there was always some obstacle in the way. Something had to be got through first, some unfinished business; time still to be served, a debt to be paid. Then life would begin. At last it dawned on me that these obstacles were my life.

Bette Howland

Friday April 4

PEOPLE from a planet without flowers would think we must be mad with joy the whole time to have such things about us.

Iris Murdoch

Saturday April 5

ONE'S life has value so long as one attributes value to the life of others, by means of love, friendship, indignation and compassion.

Simone de Beauvoir

Sunday April 6

A LMIGHTY Father, who hast given thine only Son to die for our sins, and to rise again for our justification: Grant us so to put away the leaven of malice and wickedness, that we may alway serve thee in pureness of living and truth; through the merits of the same thy Son Jesus Christ our Lord.

The Collect for the First Sunday after Easter.

The Book of Common Prayer

Monday April 7

Y ESTERDAY was a special day for us. We celebrated the fifth birthday of my great-granddaughter Bethany. In fact, her birthday falls on the first day of spring, March 21st, but Marg postponed our family party because of my absence.

Bethany, at five, is an absolutely charming little girl. She is soft-spoken and polite and yet she bubbles with enthusiasm in everything that she does.

She is quick to smile and laugh, she rarely cries, and she has a sensitivity that belies her age.

If I sound like a doting grandmother it is because I am.

I guess that my real joy is that I can see so much of my late husband George in this child and this continuation of our family gives me such happiness.

Tuesday April 8

As someone who grew up in rural eastern Canada in a farming community I came to have a great regard for the words "The Almanac says . . . ."

The Almanac to which I refer is "The Old Farmer's Almanac," a "Bible" in the farming communities across North America.

It was with great interest that I learned from Jake Frampton the early history of this still much-loved and widely-read book.

The creator and founding editor was Robert B. Thomas. Born in Grafton, Massachusetts, in 1766 to a family of well-educated farmers, his early education was in the village schools and at one of the schools of penmanship that were common at the time. His father offered to send him to college but he declined. He did continue his education in his father's library, where he first became interested in almanacs and formed a plan to produce one of his own. He found, however, that he didn't know enough mathematics to calculate the positions of the heavenly bodies on which the almanac must be based.

He enrolled in a "mathematical school" in Boston and by 1792 he was able to issue his first "Farmer's Almanac."

The first number was published in Boston but after a smallpox outbreak he moved to Sterling, Mass., where he published each year until his death in 1846.

Wednesday April 9

J OY is a net of love by which you can catch souls.

Mother Teresa

Thursday April 10

E DWARD J. McGrath, Jr. wrote in "An Exceptional View of Life":

I'm not old enough to play baseball or football. I'm not eight yet. My mom told me when you start baseball, you aren't going to be able to run that fast because you had an operation. I told Mom I wouldn't need to run that fast. When I play baseball, I'll just hit them out of the park. Then I'll be able to walk.

Friday April 11

M AVIS remarked to her granddaughter Jenna, as she came in from playing in the mud,
"You're pretty dirty, Jenna."
"I know, Grandma," she agreed, "but I'm even prettier clean."

Friday April 18

An inch of gold cannot buy an inch of time.

Chinese Proverb

Saturday April 19

As the days become longer and warmer it is more important than ever to take care of our eyes. Sunglasses, once thought to be useful but not absolutely necessary, are essential, in all seasons.

Indeed, sunglasses have become big business now that physicians have found out just how damaging the ultraviolet rays can be to our eyes.

In a recent visit to my optician I learned about the many different colours of the lenses.

Grey or green lenses are the best for general use because they are neutral tints that don't distort colour. Yellow is recommended for use in early morning or at dusk.

Pink, purple, blue and red are really fashion tints that provide little relief in bright sunlight; they will also distort colour.

Lenses that provide 100 percent u/v protection are widely recommended as are sunglasses purchased at optical stores. They are more expensive but their lenses are ground and polished and you

Saturday April 12

In California, in 1989, a landscape artist by the name of Topher Delaney discovered that she had breast cancer. After receiving the devastating news she found herself wandering the halls of the hospital looking for a place to go and think.

The only place she could find to go was the hospital cafeteria—not a very conducive place to try to pull oneself together.

She vowed right then and there that if she survived she would devote part of her landscaping practice to developing places in hospitals where people could go and process life-altering information.

After her chemotherapy, Delaney designed a meditation garden for the Kenneth Norris, Jr. Cancer Center at the University of Southern California. She then took on the task of creating a similar place of serenity in a six hundred square foot space at the Marin Cancer and Heart Institute of the Marin General Hospital in Greenbrae, California, where she had received her treatments. She equalled the $15,000 put up by the hospital with money she raised and the "Healing Garden" took shape.

Filled with plants and herbs used in the treatment of cancer and with a rock-lined stream and bright flowers, the garden provides a sanctuary for cancer patients, their families and caregivers.

It is a magnificent gesture of caring.

Sunday April 13

AND he shall be like a tree planted by the waterside: that will bring forth his fruit in due season. His leaf also shall not wither: and look, whatsoever he doeth, it shall prosper.

Psalm 1:3

Monday April 14

THE greatest sweetener of human life is Friendship. To raise this to the highest pitch of enjoyment, is a secret which but few discover.

Joseph Addison

Tuesday April 15

SURPRISINGLY, the number one thing that most people will put off till tomorrow is exercise.

In a North American poll it was found that fifty percent of adults procrastinate when it comes to working out.

I have always enjoyed walking so I find it surprising that so many will avoid exercise.

Wednesday April 16

I HAVE several friends whom I wou "serene." They are calm, happy, and r ever, flustered by anything or anyone. I e quality in a person.

Perhaps these thoughts will help you fin yourself that place where you can be peace.

Accept what comes to you totally and co so that you can appreciate it, learn fro then let it go.

Live in the present. Serene people live r the past nor in the future. Life is now.

Joy is not in things; it is in us.

Be happy with who you are and what Each of us is unique and enjoymer uniqueness brings serenity.

Thursday April 17

WHY doesn't the fellow who says speechmaker" let it go at that inst ing a demonstration?

K

Saturday April 12

IN California, in 1989, a landscape artist by the name of Topher Delaney discovered that she had breast cancer. After receiving the devastating news she found herself wandering the halls of the hospital looking for a place to go and think.

The only place she could find to go was the hospital cafeteria—not a very conducive place to try to pull oneself together.

She vowed right then and there that if she survived she would devote part of her landscaping practice to developing places in hospitals where people could go and process life-altering information.

After her chemotherapy, Delaney designed a meditation garden for the Kenneth Norris, Jr. Cancer Center at the University of Southern California. She then took on the task of creating a similar place of serenity in a six hundred square foot space at the Marin Cancer and Heart Institute of the Marin General Hospital in Greenbrae, California, where she had received her treatments. She equalled the $15,000 put up by the hospital with money she raised and the "Healing Garden" took shape.

Filled with plants and herbs used in the treatment of cancer and with a rock-lined stream and bright flowers, the garden provides a sanctuary for cancer patients, their families and caregivers.

It is a magnificent gesture of caring.

Sunday April 13

A ND he shall be like a tree planted by the waterside: that will bring forth his fruit in due season. His leaf also shall not wither: and look, whatsoever he doeth, it shall prosper.

Psalm 1:3

Monday April 14

T HE greatest sweetener of human life is Friendship. To raise this to the highest pitch of enjoyment, is a secret which but few discover.

Joseph Addison

Tuesday April 15

S URPRISINGLY, the number one thing that most people will put off till tomorrow is exercise.

In a North American poll it was found that fifty percent of adults procrastinate when it comes to working out.

I have always enjoyed walking so I find it surprising that so many will avoid exercise.

Wednesday April 16

I HAVE several friends whom I would call "serene." They are calm, happy, and rarely, if ever, flustered by anything or anyone. I envy this quality in a person.

Perhaps these thoughts will help you find within yourself that place where you can be at total peace.

Accept what comes to you totally and completely so that you can appreciate it, learn from it and then let it go.

Live in the present. Serene people live neither in the past nor in the future. Life is now.

Joy is not in things; it is in us.

Be happy with who you are and what you are. Each of us is unique and enjoyment of our uniqueness brings serenity.

Thursday April 17

W HY doesn't the fellow who says, "I'm no speechmaker" let it go at that instead of giving a demonstration?

K. Hubbard

Friday April 18

A<small>N</small> inch of gold cannot buy an inch of time.

Chinese Proverb

Saturday April 19

A<small>S</small> the days become longer and warmer it is more important than ever to take care of our eyes. Sunglasses, once thought to be useful but not absolutely necessary, are essential, in all seasons.

Indeed, sunglasses have become big business now that physicians have found out just how damaging the ultraviolet rays can be to our eyes.

In a recent visit to my optician I learned about the many different colours of the lenses.

Grey or green lenses are the best for general use because they are neutral tints that don't distort colour. Yellow is recommended for use in early morning or at dusk.

Pink, purple, blue and red are really fashion tints that provide little relief in bright sunlight; they will also distort colour.

Lenses that provide 100 percent u/v protection are widely recommended as are sunglasses purchased at optical stores. They are more expensive but their lenses are ground and polished and you won't get distortions or waves in the image that can cause headaches.

Our eyes are too valuable to jeopardize!

Sunday April 20

THE race is not to the swift, nor the battle to the strong, neither yet bread to the wise, nor yet riches to men of understanding, nor yet favour to men of skill; but time and chance happeneth to them all.

Ecclesiastes 9:11

Monday April 21

IN spite of cold and chills
That usher in the Spring,
We have the daffodils.

Tuesday April 22

IN walking, the will and the muscles are so accustomed to working together and performing their task with so little expenditure of force that the intellect is left comparatively free.

Oliver Wendell Holmes

Wednesday April 23

Back in 1993 the Baycrest Centre for Geriatric Care in Toronto introduced a Sleep Disorders program. This program was designed to help seniors cope with or solve a large range of sleeping problems.

Some of the conditions that may interfere with a good night's sleep include daytime drowsiness, snoring, nightmares or sleepwalking. Causes include minor medication addiction, pain or depression, Alzheimer's or Parkinson's diseases, or brain trauma.

This program was developed by Dr. Mortimer Mamelak, a psychiatrist who also worked with the Sleep Disorders Centre at the Sunnybrook Medical Centre in Toronto.

Although the program is open to anyone, it focuses on those 55 and over.

After discussing symptoms, patients are tested in a "sleep lab." They are placed in a small bedroom on the premises and asked to attempt napping. Four different opportunities are given at 2-hour intervals. This allows the doctor and his staff to conduct sleep latency tests while observing and recording physical movement, breathing patterns, heart rate and so on.

This program has welcomed people from as far away as New Zealand and its success rate is excellent.

We here in Canada enjoy some of the best medical services in the world.

Thursday April 24

WERE it offered to my choice, I should have no objection to a repetition of the same life from its beginning, only asking the advantage authors have in a second edition to correct some faults of the first.

Benjamin Franklin

Friday April 25

MY grandson Marshall found this item for me.

This is maturity:

To be able to stick with a job until it is finished; to be able to bear an injustice without wanting to get even; to be able to carry money without spending it; and to do one's duty without being supervised.

"You know, Gram," he said, "Mom gave these words to me when I was a teenager. At that time I was rebellious and sure that I was mature enough to be allowed to do whatever I wanted. They really hit home and I have carried this little paper in my wallet ever since then. Who knows, I may need it for my own children some day."

Saturday April 26

To carry care to bed is to sleep with a pack on your back.

Sunday April 27

To every thing there is a season, and a time to every purpose under heaven.

Ecclesiastes 3:1

Monday April 28

My thanks to the unknown author for these lines.

Let me grow lovely, growing old—
So many fine things to do:
Lace and ivory and gold
And silks need not be new.
There is a healing in old trees,
Old streets a glamour hold.
Why may not I, as well as these
Grow lovely, growing old?

Tuesday April 29

Queen Elizabeth II once called Goderich "the prettiest town in Canada." Situated on a bluff overlooking Lake Huron, Goderich has the largest harbour on the Canadian side of Lake Huron. Goderich is famous for its rock salt, an economic asset since its discovery in 1866.

Marg and I accompanied Bruce on his business trip to Goderich and while Bruce was in his meetings we had a chance to explore this interesting place.

At the centre of town is Court House Square, an octagonal park laid out in 1829 by Dr. William "Tiger" Dunlop, cofounder (with John Galt) of Goderich.

Eight tree-lined streets radiated from this park like spokes on a wheel.

During our visit we had some time to spend in the local museums. In the Huron County Pioneer Museum, housed in a 19th century school building, we saw much of Goderich's history. As well, we visited the Huron Historical Gaol and the Marine Museum, which is in the wheelhouse of a great lakes freighter.

Just a few hours from Toronto, Goderich offers a wonderful day's look at the unhurried rural Ontario of bygone days.

Wednesday April 30

To be good is noble, but to teach others how to be good is nobler—and no trouble.

Mark Twain

May

Thursday May 1

LIFE is like a garden
And friendship like a flower
That blooms and grows in beauty
With the sunshine and the shower…
And lovely are the blossoms
That are tended with great care
By those who work unselfishly
To make the place more fair…
And, like the garden blossoms,
Friendship's flower grows more sweet
When watched and tended carefully
By those we know and meet…
And, like sunshine adds new fragrance
And raindrops play their part,
Joy and sadness add new beauty
When there's friendship in the heart…
And, if the seed of friendship
Is planted deep and true
And watched with understanding,
Friendship's flower will bloom for you.

Helen Steiner Rice

Friday May 2

MY granddaughter Phyllis and I had a good laugh today when we read this list "The Way It Is" sent to her by her friend Christie.

Clearly, only a woman is skilled enough to change a toilet paper roll because no one else has ever tried it.

If you are doing anything involving tomato sauce, you should change your shirt.

If your husband asks you "Where do you keep it?" he really means he wants you to get it.

No matter how much laundry you do, the outfit your daughter absolutely has to wear is not clean.

"My mom lets me." The most common phrase uttered by a child to an adult who is not his parent. Almost always a lie.

Mothers put 30,000 kilometres a year on their cars—2 kilometres at a time.

Saturday May 3

TODAY began one of the most common rituals of spring in our area—the garage sale.

Promptly at 7:00 a.m. Bruce got in his car, armed with our local paper, and began his "pre-sale tour" of all of the garage sales in our area. Usually these sales don't begin until 8:00 a.m. but as Bruce says, "You need to be organized long before that time."

He knows that for a sale to begin at eight, families must start putting the goods out earlier.

"I take a pad of paper and I list the addresses of each sale and the interesting items at each. Then when eight o'clock finally rolls around I know exactly what I am looking for at each house and the order of their importance to me."

You would be wise to follow Bruce's regimen if you are a true garage sale aficionado. Believe me he's had years of success!

Sunday May 4

I SOUGHT to hear the voice of God
And climbed the highest steeple,
But God declared, "Go down again,
I dwell among the people."

Louis I. Newman

Monday May 5

Two of the most difficult things for us to learn are that a person can improve his financial condition by spending less and his physical condition by eating less.

Tuesday May 6

I HATE the giving of the hand unless the whole man accompanies it.

Ralph Waldo Emerson

Wednesday May 7

M Y son-in-law John is a minister. He wrote this to me in a letter some years ago.

"Some people expect their priest to have the skill in sermon composition of Knox, the oratorical power of Churchill, the personal charm of a movie star, the tact of royalty, the hide of a hippo, the administrative ability of Lord Nuffield, the wisdom of Socrates and the patience of Job. Some people must often be disappointed."

Thursday May 8

I N the Christian faith this is Ascension Day, the day that Jesus arose into Heaven.

At the service this morning we sang one of my favourite hymns. I hope you will also enjoy it.

Christ the Lord is ris'n today;
Alleluia!
Sons of men and angels say:
Alleluia!

Raise your joys and triumphs high:
Alleluia!
Sing ye heav'ns; thou earth, reply:
Alleluia!

Friday May 9

Down through the ages men and women have tried to beat the aging process. Some of their methods have been pretty strange.

In the United States in the early 1920's fundamentalist preacher John Brinkley injected crushed glands from goats and other animals into thousands of people, a very dangerous procedure.

The use of gold to fight aging originated in China in 100 B.C. A magician advised the emperor to use gold utensils and drinking goblets to achieve immortality.

At the turn of the century Nobel Prize winning scientist Elie Metchnikoff proclaimed sour milk could put a halt to aging.

Saturday May 10

Education is a private matter between the person and the world of knowledge and experience, and has little to do with school or college.

Lillian Smith

Sunday May 11

A PICTURE memory brings to me:
I look across the years and see
Myself beside my mother's knee.
I feel her gentle hand restrain
My selfish moods, and know again
A child's blind sense of wrong and pain.
But wiser now, a man gray grown,
My childhood needs are better known,
My mother's chastening love I own.

John Greenleaf Whittier

Monday May 12

ONLY those who have learned a lot are in a position to admit how little they know.

L. Carte

Tuesday May 13

BRUCE has come to be known as the master barbeque chef in our family.

One of the more popular ways to use the barbeque over the past few years has been to use meat or fish with a variety of vegetables to make "kabobs" or a delicious "dinner on a stick" as Bruce calls it.

A particular favourite of mine is Bruce's "Chicken Chomper," an easy but delicious meal.

Marinate 1 lb. boneless, skinless chicken breast pieces in 1/2 cup of any commercial Italian salad dressing for 2-3 hours.

Thread on skewers with pieces of

red onion
celery
mushrooms
blanched broccoli and cauliflower.

Because the chicken cooks quite quickly the vegetables keep an appetizing crunch.

Another easy kabob uses 1 lb. of halibut or whitefish marinated in a mixture of 1/2 cup Miracle Whip Dressing, 1 tbsp. lemon juice, 1 tsp. curry powder and threaded on a skewer with chunks of pineapple, banana and red onion.

Today we enjoyed our first of many (I hope) barbeque dinners.

Wednesday May 14

WHILE looking through an old storage box today I came across an antique album with brass-bound corners and an elegant brass clasp.

Inside the album was a collection of cards, about the size of today's business cards, that had been saved by my mother when she was young, at the turn of the century.

These cards were called "friendship cards" and they were usually quite ornate. They consisted of a bottom card in white with scalloped edges. Glued onto this card was a top card decorated with flowers, doves and friendly messages. These cards could be lifted to reveal the name of the giver printed underneath.

These lovely mementoes of friendship were most often given in person rather than sent by mail.

Some of the cards were given by Sunday school teachers as rewards for learning Bible verses.

Usually the cards were saved in albums or scrapbooks although some people chose to attach velvet ribbon and display them on bedroom or parlour walls.

Seeing them today brought back fond memories of my mother and her childhood stories.

Thursday May 15

T'IS an ill cook that cannot lick his own fingers.

William Shakespeare

Friday May 16

AT this time of year many of us are getting our gardens ready for planting.

We are fortunate to have my friend Will as an inexpensive (free) consultant ever ready to offer advice and help.

Knowing what to plant where and when is very important for a great looking garden.

For those whose thumb is slightly less green than they had hoped there is a possible answer to their prayers.

For just under twenty dollars it is possible to buy a 1 1/2-pound bag of assorted wild flower seeds. Open the bag, scatter the seeds (one bag covers 2500 square feet) and see what comes up. There are annuals and perennials in the mix so you may expect a carpet of wild flowers year after year.

A "garden in a bag" has a certain appeal, particularly to those who have little time to spend planting.

Saturday May 17

GOOD advice: Buy a used car with the same caution a naked man uses to climb a barbed-wire fence.

Sunday May 18

THE only moral lesson which is suited for a child,—the most important lesson for every time of life,—is this: "Never hurt anybody."

Jean-Jacques Rousseau

Monday May 19

IT is a glorious Monday in Muskoka on this first long weekend of the season.

Here at my friend Eleanor's cottage we have enjoyed a ski show, a magnificent display of fireworks and a bit of comic relief—Bruce's first (and unexpected) trip into the lake.

The cold dunking came as a result of Bruce's attempts to photograph the cottage from the dock. As he was focusing the camera for the perfect shot he took one backward step too many. Fortunately he kept the camera above water but it was a long time before he thawed out from his chilly dip.

Tuesday May 20

STORIES of communities working together to help one another always appeal to me. My friend Marcia related today's story in her letter from Boston.

Some years ago a young teenaged 4-H club member raised a hog especially for the junior livestock auction at the Salinas Valley Fair in King City, California. Unfortunately the young lady, a high school freshman, was in Mount Zion Hospital, San Francisco on the day of the auction, having surgery to remove a brain tumour.

Word got out the day before the auction that Nichole had gone in for surgery. The fair manager knew that there were 290 hogs so he decided to put Nichole's pig last in order to get a better price.

The arena was jammed with 800 people, all farmers from the area wanting to help this young girl and her family.

The average price for the hogs sold that day was a respectable $2.83 per pound, but as the bidding continued the price for Nichole's pig soon reached $100.00 per pound.

In an incredible outpouring of love and support, the bidding finally ended at a state-record $500.00 per pound, or $108,000.00 for the pig. As well another $8,000.00 was raised when the crowd passed around the hat.

All of the money went to defray the family's enormous medical costs. Nichole made a full recovery.

Wednesday May 21

MAY our home
Be a haven
Of peace
And contentment,
Knowing laughter
And love
Without strife;
May our home
Be a harbor
Where we find
New courage
To sail the sea
Of life.

Thanks to the author whose name is unknown.

Thursday May 22

AGE is something that doesn't matter, unless you are a cheese.

Billie Burke

Friday May 23

THE price of greatness is responsibility.

Winston Churchill

Saturday May 24

TODAY is the birthdate of Queen Victoria, one of the most beloved of all of the monarchs of England.

Born in 1819, she was just 18 years old when she took the throne after her father's death.

Her marriage to her cousin Prince Albert produced nine children.

Albert was more than the Queen's consort, taking a very active role in the management of her affairs, both public and private.

His death in 1861 left Victoria shattered and in deep mourning until the end of her life.

Victoria ruled with common sense and a forthrightness of character that allowed England to become a leader of nations, a role that this small country enjoys to this day.

Sunday May 25

THE Blessing of the Sowing

Almighty and merciful God, from whom cometh every good and perfect gift: Bless, we beseech Thee, the labours of Thy people and cause the earth to bring forth her fruits abundantly in their season, that we may with grateful hearts give thanks to Thee for the same; through Jesus Christ our Lord. Amen.

Book of Common Prayer

Monday May 26

ON Quebec's east coast there is a spectacular offshore sight at Percé, on the tip of the Gaspé Peninsula.

On Île Bonaventure, 3.5 kilometres from the beaches of Percé, is a famous bird sanctuary. From April to October tens of thousands of gannets make their home on the one hundred metre high cliffs on the island. It is the largest colony of these seabirds in the world. As well as flocks of white gannets are murres, kittiwakes, arctic puffins, cormorants, gulls and razor-billed auks.

The birds feed in the cold, shallow and nutrient-rich waters which surround the island.

During the summer there is a daily ferry service between Percé and Île Bonaventure.

Hiking trails on the island lead to lookouts where the birds and their activities can be observed at close range.

As well the island boasts an interpretive centre, a museum and many picnic sites.

It has been many years since I have visited the island but the sight of the tens of thousands of birds is not one easily forgotten.

If you are planning a visit to this beautiful area of our country this is a memorable sight to see.

Tuesday May 27

ONE of the mysteries of life
Is the magic of a tree
Unfolding in its beauty,
For all the world to see.
There's something so nostalgic
Beside a cottage door,
When lilacs bloom in springtime,
A symbol of so much more.
'Midst hues of lavender and mauve
And purple blossoms lush
A goldfinch flashes yellow bright
Flitting through the bush.
The honeybees around it swarm
To gather pollen there,

June

Sunday June 1

Love is patient, love is kind, and is not jealous; love does not brag and is not arrogant, does not act unbecomingly; it does not seek its own, is not provoked, does not take into account a wrong suffered, does not rejoice in unrighteousness, but rejoices with the truth; bears all things, believes all things, hopes all things, endures all things.

Love never fails... .

But now abide faith, hope, love, these three; but the greatest of these is love.

1 Corinthians 13:4-8, 13

These beautiful words from the Bible are a great source of comfort for me today as I remember my husband George on this, our wedding anniversary.

Monday June 2

June, by tradition, has been a month for weddings. In thinking on it the probable reason was a practical one. Planting is done in April and

Today was my day and we decided to take her boxes of old photographs and arrange them in albums according to year. Fortunately Lila had taken time before putting the pictures away to mark the dates on the back of each photo along with the names of the people and the places in each.

It was a marvellous trip down memory lane for Lila and a wonderful visual introduction to the friends and family members that I had heard about for many years.

That old adage "time flies when you're having fun" was certainly true today.

Friday May 30

WITH many wild animals at risk of extinction a game reserve in Africa has come up with an interesting program to help preserve the rare white rhinos.

"Hunters" pay several thousand dollars to go on safaris to hunt the animals but instead of bullets they shoot tranquilizing darts. A computer microchip is then inserted into the rhino's horn to help scientists track it and, on occasion, prepare the animal for transport to another game park.

This system allows both hunter and animal to enjoy a hunt with no risk to either.

Saturday May 31

MY dear friend and neighbour Lila MacGuiness and I spent a wonderful day together.

For some years now Lila has become more and more crippled by arthritis. Although she still lives in her own home, most household chores are nearly impossible for her to do on her own. The folks in our neighbourhood have set up a "calendar of help" whereby each of us takes turns signing up for different days to go to Lila's and help with whatever she needs done. Sometimes we clean windows; other times we tidy cupboards or vacuum.

The hummingbird its nectar tastes
While hovering in the air.
The delicate sweet aroma
Is wafted far and wide,
Spreading magic everywhere
In the cool of the eventide.
But all too soon the beauty sheds
Its petals at your feet,
And leaves behind a loneliness,
A haunting memory sweet.

Margaret Jewell

Wednesday May 28

PLANT and your spouse plants with you; weed and you weed alone.

Denis Breeze

Thursday May 29

A GREAT book should leave you with many experiences and slightly exhausted at the end. You live several lives while reading it.

William Styron

May and harvesting takes place from July to October for most crops.

June would be a time "between chores," so to speak, as well as a time when flowers are abundant.

For my husband George and me it was even more simple. It was the only weekend that my father, who was the minister for our service, had a day free from other ceremonies.

Tuesday June 3

IN eternity there is indeed something true and sublime. But all these times and places and occasions are now and here. God himself culminates in the present moment and will never be more divine in the lapse of the ages. Time is but a stream I go a-fishing in. I drink at it, but when I drink I see the sandy bottom and detect how shallow it is. Its thin current slides away but eternity remains.

Henry David Thoreau

Wednesday June 4

GRIEF can take care of itself; but to get the full value of a joy, you must have somebody to divide it with.

Mark Twain

Thursday June 5

THE late George Burns, comic extraordinaire, related this story many years ago in a radio interview. My husband George used it during one of his sermons.

When I was small I was singing with three other Jewish kids in our neighbourhood. A local department store had a talent contest representing all of the local churches.

The Presbyterian church had no one to enter so the minister asked if we would represent them. There we were, four Jewish boys, sponsored by the Presbyterian church and our opening song was "When Irish Eyes Are Smiling." We followed that with "Mother Machree" and won first prize. The church got a purple altar cloth and each of us got an inexpensive watch.

I raced home to tell my mother, who was hanging the wash on the roof.

"Mama, I don't want to be a Jew anymore!"

"May I ask why?" she asked calmly.

"I've been a Jew up until now and never got anything. I was a Presbyterian for fifteen minutes and I got a watch."

"First help me hang the wash—then you can be a Presbyterian."

Friday June 6

THERE is a sacredness in tears. They are not a mark of weakness, but of power. They speak more eloquently than 10,000 tongues. They are the messengers of overwhelming grief, of deep contrition and of unspeakable love.

Washington Irving

Saturday June 7

IN 1833 the *Royal William* became the first steamship to cross the Atlantic entirely on its own steam. This historic voyage marked the beginning of trans-Atlantic steam travel. The significance of this event to Canadians was that the ship set sail from Quebec City. Then after docking briefly in Pictou, Nova Scotia, it made its crossing to London, England.

The success of the *Royal William* persuaded a young shareholder in the company to build more and bigger ships. His name was Samuel Cunard.

Sunday June 8

ALL things bright and beautiful,
All creatures great and small,
All things wise and wonderful—
The Lord God made them all.

Cecil Frances Alexander

Monday June 9

Who could imagine that yet another birthday has come my way.

Like most people my age I try to ignore the occasion but family and friends seem unwilling to allow this day to go unnoticed.

Several years ago I started a tradition that I hope will continue until my passing. Instead of having people wonder, "What on earth shall we get for Edna?" I asked them to take the money that they would have used on a gift and use it to do something that they enjoy themselves. The only stipulation was that on my birthday I wanted a card that would tell me what they had done, or purchased.

This has been such fun!

This year's card was extraordinary.

My family and friends got together and bought a large number of telephone gift certificates. They then took the certificates to our local nursing home to all of the residents with cards reading "A Gift From Edna McCann."

Each of the seniors in the home now has the opportunity of making a long distance call to a loved one at absolutely no cost.

I could not have thought of a nicer gift. I confess that I was moved to tears by this gesture.

What a happy birthday this has been.

Tuesday June 10

ASPARAGUS has long been a favourite vegetable of mine. Here in Canada the home grown asparagus is particularly good but the best asparagus that I ever ate was in England.

We had spent a wonderful day sightseeing in the Cotswold hills and it was about seven o'clock before we decided that it was time to eat.

We stopped at a small, typically British place, "The Snowshill Pub."

The evening menu, written on a chalkboard at the entrance, featured Asparagus Dinner.

As far as I was concerned if it had asparagus it must be good so I ordered it, as did the rest of our group.

"Asparagus Dinner" was just that! Our plates arrived with 2 large bunches (probably about 2 lbs.) of asparagus swimming in lemon butter with hot bread and cheddar cheese.

I have never enjoyed asparagus more, before or since that occasion.

I shall try again tonight but I think perhaps the company I enjoyed probably added to the flavours.

Wednesday June 11

THE older the fiddler, the sweeter the tune.

Old English Proverb

Thursday June 12

GOD creates out of nothing. Wonderful, you say. Yes, to be sure, but he does what is still more wonderful: he makes saints out of sinners.

Sören Kierkegaard

Friday June 13

YOU, who suffer from triskadekaphobia, beware! Today is Friday the 13th and that enormous word means "a fear of the number 13 when it appears on a Friday."

For those of us who are less superstitious it is simply another beautiful day to enjoy.

Saturday June 14

WHEN something goes wrong it is important to talk not about who is to blame but who is going to fix it.

Sunday June 15

EACH little flow'r that opens,
Each little bird that sings,
He made their glowing colours,
He made their tiny wings.

Verse 2

Cecil Frances Alexander

Monday June 16

Bruce and Marshall have spent some time golf-ing together in the past few weeks. Both men enjoy the game but they don't play to the exclusion of all else in their lives. Having heard many stories of "golf widows" I thought you might enjoy Marshall's joke of today.

A golf foursome was playing on a course where the first three holes parallel the road. As the group walked down the third fairway, a limousine drove along the road and then stopped. Out jumped a beautiful girl in full wedding array.

"John, John," she sobbed, throwing her arms around one of the players. "Why have you left me waiting at the church?"

"Now, now, Nicole," he said sternly, "Remember I said 'if it rained'!"

Tuesday June 17

So long as enthusiasm lasts, so long is youth still with us.

Wednesday June 18

Rudyard Kipling, celebrated British author and Nobel prize-winner endured much criticism of his work before his books gained popularity.

In 1910 Kipling penned the poem "If" for his 12-year-old son, and included it in a book of children's tales.

Critics did not consider it to be one of his great works, yet within a few years the poem became a classic world-wide, translated into 27 languages.

Here are 2 verses of "If."

If you can keep your head when all about you
Are losing theirs and blaming it on you,
If you can trust yourself when all men doubt
    you,
But make allowance for their doubting too;
If you can wait and not be tired by waiting,
Or being lied about, don't deal in lies,
Or being hated, don't give way to hating,
And yet don't look too good, nor talk too wise:

If you can talk with crowds and keep your
    virtue,
Or walk with Kings—nor lose the common
    touch,
If neither foes nor loving friends can hurt you,
If all men count with you, but none too much;
If you can fill the unforgiving minute
With sixty seconds' worth of distance run,
Yours is the Earth and everything that's in it,
And—which is more—you'll be a Man, my son!

Thursday June 19

My friends Muriel and Will stopped in today so that Will could make certain that his handiwork in our garden was being well cared for.

Muriel was wearing a calamine-like lotion around her eyes.

"You know, Edna, I thought that this rash was poison ivy. I was quite surprised when the doctor told me that it probably came from the flowers in our garden.

"When I'm working with the flowers I often get hot and I wipe my face with the back of my hand or my wrist, both of which have been in contact with the flowers.

"Surprisingly, very common flowers such as tulips, chrysanthemums, philodendrons and spider ferns can cause the rash.

"Of course, the best way to prevent the rash is to avoid touching exposed skin while gardening.

"Washing your hands when finished will also help."

This is a word of warning for you gardening enthusiasts: all that itches may not be poison ivy.

Friday June 20

The bridges that you cross before you come to them are over rivers that aren't there.

Gene Brown

Saturday June 21

TODAY begins summer, my favourite season of the year. I offer "Summer Song" by E. Nesbit to welcome the season.

There are white moon daisies in the midst of
    the meadow
Where the flowered grass scatters its seeds like
    spray,
There are purple orchis by the wood-ways'
    shadow
There are pale dog-roses by the white highway;
And the grass, the grass is tall, the grass is up
    for hay,
With daisies white like silver and the buttercups
    like gold,
And it's oh! for once to play thro' the long, the
    lovely day,
To laugh before the year grows old!
There is silver moonlight on the breast of the
    river
Where the willows tremble to the kiss of night,
Where the nine tall aspens in the meadow
    shiver,
Shiver in the night wind that turns them white.
And the lamps, the lamps are lit, the lamps are
    glow-worms' light,
Between the silver aspens and the west's last
    gold.

And it's oh! to drink delight in the lovely lonely
 night,
To be young before the heart grows old!

Sunday June 22

FATHER'S DAY

So many of the things that we get from our fa-
thers are intangible, things we sometimes can't
quite put our finger on until we are much older.

When I remember my father I marvel at his
calm acceptance of everything that came his way.

If some particularly vexing problem was both-
ering him he would look at it in a quiet manner
with logic and reason. He would give thought before acting and more often than not the problem
would be resolved.

Any emergency became less urgent under father's quiet response.

He lived by the words "everything happens for
the best" and we children came to accept this as
true.

On this Father's Day I remember my own father with love and a thankful spirit for all that he
gave to me.

Monday June 23

TELL me who admires you and I will tell you who you are.

C.A. Sainte-Beuve

Tuesday June 24

ST. JEAN BAPTISTE DAY

OUR French Canadian friends celebrate this day with unbridled enthusiasm. Family get-togethers with traditional tourtière pies and the waving of the blue and white fleur-de-lis flags all give a wonderful sense of the French heritage that has given so much to our great country.

Wednesday June 25

THE greatest happiness of life is the conviction that we are loved, loved for ourselves, or rather loved in spite of ourselves.

Victor Hugo

Thursday June 26

ACHES and pains are your body's way of telling you something. As you grow older your body becomes more and more talkative.

Friday June 27

THIS is a wonderful time of year to try some of the marvellous cold drinks that refresh us. One of my favourites is called Ice Cap.

Dissolve 1/4 cup instant coffee in an equal amount of boiling water and 1/4 cup sugar or low-calorie sweetener to taste.

Stir in 4 cups of milk and add ice. This makes 6 servings and is guaranteed to refresh.

Saturday June 28

I NEVER see a garden anywhere
That I do not see God walking there.

Sunday June 29

THE purple-headed mountain,
The river running by,
The sunset, and the morning
That brightens up the sky.
The cold wind in the winter,
The pleasant summer sun,
The ripe fruits in the garden,
He made them every one.

Verses 3, 4

C.F. Alexander

Monday June 30

My granddaughter Phyllis and her family stopped in for a visit today. The twins, Justin and Jenny, are finished school for this year and looking forward to the summer holiday.

Today they went for a hike along a very interesting trail in the Caledon area. In the 1870's it was built as the Hamilton Northwestern Railway to join Hamilton with Barrie and Collingwood. Later it became part of the Grand Trunk then the CNR before it was phased out of the line a little more than twenty years ago.

The Town of Caledon bought the right-of-way for the bargain price of $30,000 in 1989. It is now the Caledon Trailway, stretching from Terra Cotta northeast past Palgrave.

This is an ideal trail for walking, biking or even horseback riding. The trail follows a glacial spillway where meltwaters gouged out a nearly level valley at the end of the last ice age.

There are seven trestle bridges over streams and valleys, all equipped with handrails.

July

Tuesday July 1

CANADA DAY

O CANADA! Our home and native land!
True patriot love in all thy sons command.
With glowing hearts we see thee rise,
The True North strong and free!
From far and wide, O Canada,
We stand on guard for thee.
God keep our land glorious and free!
O Canada, we stand on guard for thee.
O Canada, we stand on guard for thee!

The history of this, our national anthem, is an interesting story.

In 1880, when O Canada was composed, the country was still dependent on Britain and the anthem was "God Save the Queen." In spring of that year the St. Jean Baptiste Society of Quebec organized a festival for French-speaking people from all across North America. A music committee of the Society decided that a song was needed.

Calixa Lavallée, a Quebec musician, composed the music and Adolphe-Basile Routhier wrote the verses in French. The official premiere was June 24, St. Jean Baptiste Day, 1880.

In 1908, in a competition organized by Collier's Weekly, the words of Robert Weir came to be those of the official English anthem.

In 1967 the words were amended to those which we now sing with love and enthusiasm.

O CANADA

Wednesday July 2

MY great grandson Justin is interested in animals.

Here are some of the unusual facts that he found in a library book this week.

Beavers were once the size of bears.

Seventy million years ago whales walked on the earth. The modern whale has evolved from a land creature with legs and whales' bodies still have the remnants of hip bones.

Ancient penguins once stood about five feet tall and weighed about three hundred pounds—more than three times the weight of today's largest, the emperor penguin.

Elephants, living on islands in the Mediterranean, were once the size of pigs.

Thursday July 3

THE best and most beautiful things in the world cannot be seen or even touched. They must be felt with the heart.

Helen Keller

Friday July 4

FOURTH of July Celebrations

Let there be prayers as well as great parades,
Let hymns combine with patriotic songs,
Let there be leaders of the future days,
With heroes of the past amid the throngs.
Let reverent silence punctuate the noise,
Let God be praised for this great land of ours,
Let sober meditation balance joys
And grave humility mark crucial hours.
Let statesmanship grow from this nation's need.
Let citizenship be equal to these days
That godly men who gave their lives indeed
Be not betrayed by dull, indifferent ways.
Let joyfulness, not wildness, mark the Free,
That God may find us worth our liberty!

Thanks to Betty W. Stoffel.

I wish to my many friends in the United States a Happy Fourth of July.

Saturday July 5

ACCORDING to my son-in-law Bruce, one of the quickest ways to meet new people is to pick up the wrong ball on a golf course.

Sunday July 6

DEAR Friends, let us love one another, because love is from God. Everyone who loves is a child of God and knows God.

1 John 4:7

Monday July 7

AN author whose works I have enjoyed lately is Anna Quindlen.

Anna, a young woman living in northern New Jersey, has enjoyed much success early in her career. Her first novel, *Object Lessons*, was a best seller. Her *New York Times* column "Public and Private" won a Pulitzer Prize in 1992 and a selection of these columns was published as *Thinking Out Loud*. She is also the author of a collection of her "Life In The 30's" columns, *Living Out Loud*, and a children's book *The Tree That Came To Stay.*

What I admire most about Anna Quindlen is her extraordinary intelligence, humour and insight. She has great depth in her perceptions about the public and private lives of ordinary people.

I have enjoyed her works immensely and I recommend them as excellent reading to those of you who may not have had the pleasure of getting to know this fine young writer.

Tuesday July 8

WHAT I love most at this time of year is the abundance of fresh fruit and vegetables. We are enjoying the large red strawberries, freshly picked and delicious. Soon the blueberries, tomatoes, peas, beans and corn will be ripe and ready to be harvested for our eating pleasure.

What a difference today's refrigerators and freezers have made in the way we are able to enjoy these foods.

When I was young we ate the food in season but we spent hours and hours canning for winter. Some foods like apples and potatoes were kept in the fruit cellars and they often lasted almost all winter.

Now, with our ability to quick-freeze many

fruits and vegetables, we are able to enjoy "fresh-picked" flavour and goodness in all seasons.

As well our supermarkets offer a wide variety of fruits and vegetables year round at a reasonable cost.

When I think back on the years of hard work that my grandmothers, mother and I endured in the name of healthy eating, today's methods of buying, cooking and storing seem all that much more remarkable.

How I wish my own mother could have enjoyed it as well.

Wednesday July 9

TODAY was our double celebration day—Phyllis and Bill's anniversary, and Justin and Jenny's birthday. It hardly seems possible that it was twelve years ago today that we were looking at two little bundles, so tiny that they looked like dolls. Thanks to the excellent care given by the hospital staff these two youngsters are, today, the picture of good health.

It's interesting to see that Jenny has grown quickly in the past couple of months and is now slightly taller than Justin. Justin views this philosophically.

"It's okay that Jenny's taller right now, Gran. Every girl in our class is taller than us boys but wait till next year. Dad thinks I'm going to be more than six feet tall so I bet I'll outgrow Jenny by a lot!"

I know that my husband George would have been proud to see what wonderful great-grandchildren our family has produced. I know that family was so important to him.

Thursday July 10

IF you want to stay young, associate with young people; if you want to feel your age, try to keep up with them.

Friday July 11

SOMETIMES it helps to know that I just can't do it all. One step at a time is all that's possible— even when those steps are taken on the run.

A.W. Schaef

Saturday July 12

ONE of the most enjoyable ways to relive any vacation is to pull out the picture albums and see once again the people and places that you enjoyed.

My friend Mary showed me a wonderful way to make your vacation album just a little more special.

Using a roadmap and white glue, cover a spiral-bound photo album. Align one side of the map to the holes and wrap the other 3 edges to the inside and glue.

With a marker or paint, retrace your route on the map and let it dry.

On a small piece of coloured paper, print "My Vacation" with a marker.

Using one photograph from the vacation, centre and glue the photo on a piece of craft foam 3 inches square and 1/8" thick. Glue to the map cover.

A small plastic toy car or plane may be glued on to complete this unique album.

Sunday July 13

IF I take the wings of the morning and settle at the farthest limits of the sea, even there shall your hand lead me, and your right hand shall hold me fast.

Psalm 139:9-10

Monday July 14

NORMAL day, let me be aware of the treasure you are. Let me learn from you, love you, bless you before you depart. Let me not pass you by in quest of some rare and perfect tomorrow. Let me hold you while I may, for it may not always be so.

Mary Jean Iron

Tuesday July 15

I T does seem so pleasant to talk with an old acquaintance who knows what you know. I see so many new folks nowadays who seem to have neither past nor future. Conversation has got to have some root in the past, or else you have got to explain every remark you make, and it wears a person out.

Sarah Orne Jewett

Wednesday July 16

A S I listened to the baseball game tonight the name Mickey Mantle was mentioned several times. I was not a fan of baseball at the time Mickey Mantle was a star but I learned about this man at the time of his death in August of 1995.

Mickey Mantle emerged from poverty in Commerce, Oklahoma, when he signed with the New York Yankees in 1949. His father Elvin ("Mutt") had drilled his son hours a day teaching him to hit both right- and left-handed. He was called up to the majors in 1951 where he was an astonishing blend of power and speed.

In his 18-year career he hit 536 home runs and, though constantly hobbled by injuries, he led the Yankees to seven world championships.

Despite his "star" status he was plagued by self-doubt and he became an alcoholic at an early age. This battle with alcohol continued until 1994 when he entered the Betty Ford Center for treatment of his alcoholism.

In June 1995 he underwent a liver transplant operation. At first it seemed to be a success but then it was found that the cancer had spread and was swiftly overwhelming his body.

Before his death he managed to coin the slogan "Be a hero, be a donor." His efforts for the donor program may make him as great a star after his death as he was in his playing heyday.

Thursday July 17

WHEN someone does a kindness
  It always seems to me
That's the way God up in heaven
  Would like us all to be . . .
For when we bring some pleasure
  To another human heart,
We have followed in His footsteps
  And we've had a little part

In serving Him who loves us—
    For I am very sure it's true
That in serving those around us
    We serve and please Him, too.

Helen Steiner Rice

Friday July 18

M Y friend Jake Frampton gave this advice on fishing to his young nephew.

"When you go fishing, look for an old man. He has more time to figure out where the 'holes' are and when he has his line full and leaves, you take his place."

His nephew reported that the last time he saw a white-haired man fishing in an unlikely spot he took his place and returned with his limit.

Saturday July 19

B RUCE and Marshall enjoyed playing golf at a local course today. Although many of the private clubs are expensive to join, it is still possible to find reasonably priced places to play this very popular game.

Anyone wanting to play golf in the early days of this century might have had to create a course.

The established courses were few and far between, usually located near big cities or resorts, and they catered to the wealthy.

For those would-be players deprived of country club links, a cow pasture often provided a chance to play. It was referred to as "petty links."

These early players were often assisted in their endeavours by a 1903 book titled *How to Play Golf on a Five-Acre Meadow.*

Pasture players soon learned that the farther one drove the ball the more difficult it was to find in the long meadow grass.

A sea captain named Wright fashioned a ball from hard white pine that lofted beautifully but didn't travel far enough to get lost. These wooden "dead-balls" rarely travelled over 50 feet. Course layouts in the book described fairways ranging from 60 yards down to only 33.

For many early golfers "petty links" and "dead-ball golf" were the beginning of golf's first steps away from the exclusive country clubs of the wealthy.

Sunday July 20

SOME friends play at friendship, but a true friend sticks closer than one's nearest kin.

Proverbs 18:24

Monday July 21

YOUTH is happy because it has the ability to see beauty. Anyone who keeps the ability to see beauty never grows old.

Franz Kafka

Tuesday July 22

OUR neighbourhood is quiet at this time of year. Many of the youngsters are off at camp or away with friends or family at summer cottages.

If you know any children who are off at camp one of the nicest things that you can do is to send postcards or letters. No matter what their age children love to get mail when they are away from home. On occasion, a letter may relieve homesickness and make their stay more enjoyable.

Wednesday July 23

TODAY is another special day in our family. On this day forty-five years ago a very young couple stood nervously at the front of a small church and repeated their wedding vows. Now, all these years later, Marg and Bruce are even happier and more in love.

Bruce was reflecting on their marriage today and I think he summed up their life together very well.

"You know, Mother, Marg and I are very lucky. We've been blessed with wonderful children and grandchildren. Our family unit with parents, aunts, uncles, and cousins is strong and supportive.

"But most important is that Marg and I have developed a wonderful friendship together. Some people may not realize that friendship is the strongest foundation for a marriage."

Whatever their secret is, I know that their life together has been a joy and we all wish for them another 40 years of happiness.

Thursday July 24

FEW things can brighten feminine eyes
More than getting into a smaller size.

Friday July 25

AFTER all is said and done, no matter how famous or important a man may be, the size of his funeral is going to depend a lot on the weather.

Saturday July 26

BACK in 1995, when Jeanne Calment celebrated her 120th birthday in Arles, France, people marvelled at the changes she had seen in her lifetime.

When she was born, Victor Hugo was still alive. Vincent Van Gogh came to her native Arles to paint when she was just 13.

The invention of the telephone, the automobile, the airplane and the use of electric power were a part of the future in her life.

When someone asked her on her birthday what kind of future she expected her reply was "Short, very short."

Sunday July 27

TAKE care that you do not despise one of these little ones; for I tell you, in heaven their angels continually see the face of my Father.

Matthew 18:10

Monday July 28

ALL parents believe their children can do the impossible. They thought it the minute we were born, and no matter how hard we've tried to prove them wrong, they all think it about us now. And the really annoying thing is, they're probably right.

Cathy Guisewite

Tuesday July 29

IF you think your talents are too insignificant to be effective, then you've never been in bed with a mosquito.

Wednesday July 30

THE marvellous richness of human experience would lose something of rewarding joy if there were no limitations to overcome. The hilltop hour would not be half so wonderful if there were no dark valleys to traverse.

Helen Keller

Thursday July 31

MARG pulled out an old magazine today and in it we saw an advertisement for paper dresses! How many of you remember that strange time back in the 1960's when paper dresses became the rage?

Developed by the Scott Paper Company and offered by mail for the bargain price of $1.25, they were originally a promotion for a line of towels and toilet tissue. The promotion caught on so well that soon dress manufacturers came up with more elaborate designs.

At one time a company was selling 80,000 paper dresses a week. *Time Magazine* wrote in 1967, "Paper clothing apparently is here to stay."

Experts predicted that within ten years most of the world would be wearing disposable clothing.

However, as is often the case when "experts" are involved, paper clothing proved to be just another passing fad.

August

Friday August 1

THIS is the hay that no man planted,
This is the ground that was never plowed
Watered by tides, cold and brackish,
Shadowed by fog and the sea-born cloud.

This is the crop above which sounded
No bobolink's song, but the gull's long cry,
That men now reap as they reap their meadows
And mound in the great gold stacks to dry.

In the long winter months when deep pile the
    snowdrifts
And the cattle stand in the dusk all day
Many a cow shall taste pale seaweed
Twined in the stalks of the wild salt hay.

Elizabeth Coatsworth

Saturday August 2

ONE of the scientific marvels of our time, in
vitro fertilization, is also proving to be a problem from time to time.

The marvel, of course, is that couples who would have remained childless years ago are able now to have a family.

The problem is that sometimes mistakes are made in the hospitals that are providing the fertilization process.

In the Netherlands a bizarre mix-up took place when a technician accidentally reused a glass tube to collect sperm from the husband of a hopeful mother-to-be. The white couple gave birth to twin boys, one of whom was white and the other black.

The parents love both children dearly as any parents would but the children have been the target of many racist remarks.

Thankfully such mix-ups are extremely rare but there are doctors who have refused to participate in any of the fertilization programs for fear of repercussions at a later date.

I'm sure that such decisions must be extremely difficult for those people involved in trying to balance the desire to help the childless and the need to protect themselves in a profession that provides the opportunity for disastrous errors.

Sunday August 3

THE kingdom of God is not coming with things that can be observed; nor will they say to you, "Look, here it is!" or "There it is!" For, in fact, the kingdom of God is among you.

Luke 17:20-21

Monday August 4

THE sun drew off at last his piercing fires.
Over the stale warm air, dull as a pond
And moveless in the gray quieted street,
Blue magic of a summer evening glowed.

Lascelles Abercrombie

Tuesday August 5

NOTHING reminds a woman of something she wants done so much as seeing her husband sitting down.

Wednesday August 6

MY daughter Mary and her husband John are on a road trip through the northeastern United States. In their letter today they told us of their time spent in the beautiful ski-town of Stowe, Vermont.

"Because Stowe is so often associated with winter skiing, the visitors association provides a list of inexpensive activities to do in Stowe and the surrounding areas.

"Yesterday we walked the eight-kilometre recreation path that winds through and around this beautiful village.

"Today we drove on the twisting route through Smugglers Notch, another ski area, on the narrow mountain pass that was used for smuggling livestock to Canada during the War of 1812.

"Our favourite activity to date was the tour of the Ben and Jerry's ice cream factory which is located 15 minutes south of town. For just one dollar we had a half-hour tour of the factory and then we sampled the 'flavour of the day,' cookie dough and chocolate.

"I never realized that this area was so beautiful in the summer as well as in the winter.

"Our next stop is Middlebury, Vermont, a beautiful college town that boasts the Middlebury Inn, one of the oldest inns in America."

Thursday August 7

IF you tell a man there are three hundred billion stars, he will believe you.

If you tell him a bench has just been painted, he has to touch it to be sure.

Friday August 8

MY daughter Julia is a "clutter-bug." Perhaps because she travels so much and is rarely at

home for any length of time her house often becomes burdened with items that she no longer
needs or uses.

This weekend she has decided to change this
with the "four-container method" recommended
to her by a friend.

In this system you start in one room. The first
box is for anything that belongs to another room,
such as the garden trowel that somehow wound up
in your bedroom.

The second box is for things you never use but
are too good to throw away. Donate them to char-
ity or sell them.

The third box is for items you can't make your
mind up about keeping, selling or throwing away.

A trash can is the fourth and most important
container. Throw out what you don't need!

At the end of the day at least some things will
be gone—she hopes.

Saturday August 9

I HAVE made my annual trek to Muskoka to visit
with my dear friend Eleanor. Each year that I
return to this magnificent area I am astonished
anew at its incredible beauty. The crystal clear
water, the tall pines swaying gently in the breeze
and the majestic rock formations combine to provide a beauty unrivalled in any area that I know.

Tonight Eleanor and I enjoyed our tea on the Muskoka chairs on the dock. Is there anything nicer than a good cup of tea shared with a friend on a beautiful summer's evening? I don't think so.

Sunday August 10

WE sang this old favourite hymn at church this morning.

Blest be the tie that binds
Our hearts in Jesus' love;
The fellowship of Christian minds
Is like to that above.

When for a while we part,
This thought will soothe our pain;
That we shall be joined in heart,
And one day meet again.

Rev. John Fawcett

Monday August 11

NOTHING is work unless you'd rather be doing something else.

Tuesday August 12

For many cottagers in the Muskoka area no summer would be complete without a trip to Port Carling and a visit to the Indian Village of craft shops.

Years ago the riverbank was crowded with dozens of tiny cabins selling the Indian wares. Today there is but one of these shops open yet the shelves are almost invisible under handwoven baskets, deerskin moccasins, hand-knit sweaters and birchbark picture frames and tiny canoes.

The Indians who run the shop come from Gibson Indian Reserve close to Bala, and it is on the reserve, during the winter, that they work to replenish their stock for summer sale.

The pride in their native heritage is evident in the exquisite work that makes each item unique.

It is to be hoped that the young people of the reserve will learn the skills of their ancestors and that these crafts will be available for generations to come.

Wednesday August 13

God never loved me in so sweet a way before.
'Tis He alone who can such blessing send.
And when His love would new expressions find,

He brought thee to me and He said—"Behold a friend."

Thursday August 14

THERE is a serene and settled majesty to woodland scenery that enters into the soul and delights and elevates it, and fills it with noble inclinations.

Washington Irving

Friday August 15

WHAT does he who plants a tree?
He plants the friend of sun and sky;
He plants the flag of breezes free;
The shaft of beauty towering high.

Henry C. Bunner

Saturday August 16

DURING the summer here in Muskoka there are numerous arts and crafts shows to enjoy each weekend.

Eleanor and I attended one of those shows today and we were impressed with the quality and variety of articles presented by the talented artisans.

Some of the work I liked most was a variety of wooden handicrafts from the "Muskoka Loonatic."

The "Loonatic" is really Rod Botterill, a school teacher from Belleville. Several years ago Rod began carving and painting loons of various sizes. From there he branched out into welcome boards for cottages with the loons cut out and painted, then glued to the boards. His wife, Leslie, also a school teacher and a talented artist, joined her husband in creating unique items, each hand-painted and beautifully finished.

Barnboard and other wooden birdhouses are very popular items as are their pine garbage containers, large enough to hold the big green garbage bags and decorated with a painting of the historic steamer *Segwun* or a variety of Muskoka wildlife.

This talented couple are enjoying much deserved success with their "other" careers.

Sunday August 17

TAKE my yoke upon you and learn from me; for I am gentle and humble in heart, and you will find rest for your souls. For my yoke is easy, and my burden is light.

Matthew 11:29-30

Monday August 18

THE best way to get your tomatoes to ripen is to go on vacation. The tomatoes will sense your absence, ripen, rot and fall to the ground before you get back—even if you are gone only two days.

Fred H. Keller

Tuesday August 19

WHEN you teach your son, you teach your son's son.

The Talmud

Wednesday August 20

ELEANOR was having a dinner party this evening—just a small group of neighbours and friends here at the cottage.

Unfortunately, we were enjoying reading on the porch and neither of us remembered that the roast was in the oven cooking. The smell of smoke was the first indication of a disaster in the kitchen.

Fortunately, Eleanor was able to cut off the few overcooked areas and the guests were none the wiser as she cut up the remaining meat and made a delicious stir-fry with fresh vegetables.

Actually, Eleanor told her guests of the near-disaster and they had some other suggestions for saving seemingly ruined foods.

Stews or gravies that are too salty can be saved by thinly slicing a raw potato and cooking the slices in the stews or gravies until slices are translucent. Potatoes will absorb the extra salt. Remove and discard the slices.

You can save dry turkey or chicken by slicing the meat and arranging it on a heatproof platter. Make a sauce of half each melted butter and chicken broth. Pour over the turkey or chicken slices and let the dish stand in a 250° oven for ten minutes. The meat will soak up the sauce and become juicy again.

Thursday August 21

IN a perfect world pro baseball players would complain about teachers being paid contracts worth millions of dollars.

John Gratton

Friday August 22

IF you can't have the best of everything, make the best of everything you have.

Saturday August 23

A SMOOTH sea never made a skilful mariner.

Sunday August 24

NEW every morning is the love
Our wakening and uprising prove:
Through sleep and darkness safely brought,
Restored to life, and power, and thought.

Rev. John Keble

Monday August 25

WHAT a delightful stay I had in Muskoka.
Time spent with old and cherished friends
is some of the best time that we can enjoy in this
lifetime.

Keep up your friendships—as we age we have
more need of friends than ever before.

Tuesday August 26

THIS is a fish story guaranteed to amuse.

A sixty-year-old Amsterdam fisherman became
seasick on an outing in the North Sea.

As he leaned over the side of the boat his bottom plate fell from his mouth and sank.

In November of the same year a tackle shop owner was helping to clean fish caught from the same charter boat. Inside a cod he was surprised to find a set of false teeth.

The captain of the boat remembered the fisherman's lost teeth, and the teeth and the owner were reunited.

Said the fisherman, "I don't mind where they've been. A cod's stomach is very clean."

Wednesday August 27

THE day will come when, after harnessing space, the winds, the tides and gravitation, we shall harness for God the energies of love. And on that day, for the second time in the history of the world, we shall have discovered fire.

Tielhard de Chardin

Thursday August 28

EXPERIENCE is not what happens to a man. It is what a man does with what happens to him.

Aldous Huxley

Thursday September 4

THERE is a very old book by Anna Robertson Brown, an 1833 graduate of Wellesley College. This thin volume is titled *What Is Worth While?* and as I read it today I marvelled at the relevance of her insights in today's world.

In the opening lines of her book she writes, "One life to live! We all want to make the most of it. How can we accomplish the most with the energies and powers at our command? What is worthwhile?"

These are questions that we may all ask ourselves.

"We may let go all things which we cannot carry into eternal life."

The things that she suggests we should let go are pretence, "Eternity is not for shams"; worry, "It is spiritual nearsightedness, a way of looking at little things and magnifying their value"; discontent, "Make a heroic life out of whatever is set before us"; and self-seeking, "In eternal life there is no greed."

Those things to keep, she suggests, are wise use of time, vital work, daily happiness, love, friendship and faith.

People like Anna accept dying as a natural progression because they believe life has meaning.

Her insightful words were uplifting for me today.

Tuesday September 2

IN most areas this is the "First Day of School." Marg and I enjoyed watching the youngsters in our neighbourhood as they walked, skipped, ran, or were pulled reluctantly by the hand toward our local halls of learning.

Most children are quite happy to be back at school because it allows them to renew friendships that are often on hold during the summer due to vacations.

As well, most children thrive on the structure that school gives to their daily lives. Vacations are an enjoyable part of any life but structure and organization provide the security that all children, and adults, need.

Wednesday September 3

THE clock of life is wound but once,
And no man has the power
To tell just when the hands will stop,
At late or early hour.
Now is the only time you own,
Live, love, toil with a will,
Place no faith in "tomorrow" for
The clock may then be still.

Friday August 29

A N optimist is a person who leaves the dishes because he thinks he will feel more like doing them in the morning.

Saturday August 30

A LL across the country people are enjoying this last long weekend of the summer season.

How quickly the warm days have passed—the evenings have that bit of chill that heralds the coming of autumn.

Enjoy these days! Too soon it will be winter.

Sunday August 31

J ESUS said unto Martha, "I am the resurrection and the life: He that believeth in me, though he were dead, yet shall he live."

John 11:25

September

Monday September 1

THIS is the day each year when we honour the workers of our country. I offer you ideas of work, both old and new.

Choose a job you love and you will never have to work a day in your life.

Confucius

I never did anything worth doing by accident, nor did any of my inventions come by accident; they came by work.

Thomas A. Edison

Work is love made visible.

Kahlil Gibran

Friday September 5

A REALLY contented person has his yesterdays all filed away, his present in order, and his tomorrow subject to instant revision.

Saturday September 6

WHATEVER is worth doing at all is worth doing well.

Philip Chesterfield

My father used this quotation very often when we were children. He lived his own life by this philosophy and he made a great effort to instill this sense of purpose in us.

George and I in our turn tried to pass it along to our girls and again it passed to the next generation.

I have heard Phyllis use this phrase and I know that she will expect a first-class effort from the twins—just as she expects it from herself.

Sunday September 7

ONE day is with the Lord as a thousand years, and a thousand years as one day.

II Peter 3:8

Monday September 8

Wɪᴛʜ the children back in classrooms all across the country I felt that this prayer for teachers would be appropriate.

Grant we beseech thee, O heavenly Father, to all who teach in our schools, the spirit of wisdom and grace, that they may lead their pupils to reverence truth, desire goodness and rejoice in beauty; so that all may come to know and worship thee, the giver of all that is good; through Jesus Christ our Lord.

Tuesday September 9

Aᴜᴛᴜᴍɴ is fast approaching and the signs are everywhere. There is a nip in the evening air that wasn't there a few short weeks ago. Here and there trees have leaves that are picking up the red, gold and brown colours of fall.

In our town we have seen the most certain signs of the season changing—the football teams are practising and the cross-country runners race by in their school team shirts.

Wednesday September 10

A ᴄᴏᴜɴᴛʀʏ that has long fascinated me is Australia. Australia has been described as a nation of wide-open spaces, outgoing people and strange, marvellous animals.

The original inhabitants of Australia, the Aborigines, migrated there from Southeast Asia more than 40,000 years ago, probably clinging to primitive rafts and walking over a partial land bridge. These skilled hunters set bush fires to flush game and encourage the growth of new shoots—food for the animals. Their nomadic lifestyle minimized adverse effects on the environment.

Just 200 years ago the Europeans arrived.

"The finest harbour in the world" was the praise given by British Captain Arthur Phillip to Sydney Cove. It was here that he founded the continent's first European settlement.

Australia today is a mecca for tourists. From the unique architecture of the Opera House in Sydney to the incredible ecosystem of The Great Barrier Reef, from the spectacular scenery of the south to the parched empty outback at the centre of the continent, tourists flock here by the millions.

Want to see kangaroos and koalas? Australia is the place for you.

Thursday September 11

SAYING yes to a child is like blowing up a balloon. You have to know when to stop.

Friday September 12

AT this time of year people are readying their homes for the coming of winter. Unhappily it is a time of year when unscrupulous home repair contractors are able to take advantage of the unwary.

Here are a few suggestions of "danger signs" to watch for when you are considering hiring a contractor.

1. Beware of the promise of a great price if you allow your home to be used for advertising purposes.
2. Be wary of companies that use a post office box with no street address or phone number.
3. Salespersons who pressure you to sign a contract with scare tactics like "this price is available only if you sign today" are usually suspect.
4. Contractors who do not offer references should be carefully checked.
5. If payment in full is required before work is done you should be wary.

Remember, if it sounds too good to be true, it probably is.

Saturday September 13

HAVE you ever noticed how unevenly patience is distributed on the highway? The driver ahead of you always has too much, and the one behind you has too little.

Sunday September 14

AT this time of harvest this joyful hymn of
thanks is often sung.
Come, ye thankful people, come.
Raise the song of harvest-home!
All is safely gathered in,
Ere the winter storms begin.
God, our Maker, doth provide
For our wants to be supplied;
Come to God's own temple, come,
Raise the song of harvest-home!

Monday September 15

THE harvest of old age is the recollection and
abundance of blessing previously secured.

Marcus Tullius Cicero

Tuesday September 16

THE vegetables at the farmers' markets are su-
perb right now. Coming from Canada's east
coast, one of my favourite vegetables is the potato.
I offer you today a delicious casserole using this
most popular of vegetables.

8 large red potatoes (about 3 lbs.)
6 medium red onions (about 1 1/2 lbs.)

2 tablespoons olive or salad oil
1 1/2 teaspoons salt (optional)
1 teaspoon coarsely ground black pepper
1 teaspoon dried thyme leaves
1 tablespoon dried parsley

1. Preheat oven to 425°. Cut each potato into quarters. Cut each onion lengthwise in half, keeping the skin and root end on.
2. In a large roasting pan (about 12" x 17") toss the potatoes and onions with olive or salad oil, salt, pepper, dried thyme and parsley until the vegetables are well coated. Roast vegetables 45 minutes, turning them with a spatula once or twice until golden and fork tender.
3. Arrange potatoes and onions on a warm large platter. Serves 6 as an accompaniment.

This is also delicious when refrigerated and served cold.

Wednesday September 17

MICKEY Heinecken, coach of the Middlebury College Panthers football team, is one of those rarities in the sport—a man who believes that displaying a graceful attitude is more important than winning or losing.

In 1995 when asked about his most memorable moment in Middlebury football he told about a loss from his fourth season of coaching.

"One of my proudest moments as a coach came in my fourth season. We were undefeated going into the last game against Norwich. We lost in a very tight and traumatic game. Roy Heffernan, who is one of the best running backs we've ever had, came into the locker room. All these kids had their heads down, and Roy had torn a cartilage in his knee in the first half, and finished the game despite needing surgery. He said, 'Hey guys, I've got tears in my eyes, too, but I hope your tears are for the same reason mine are. We just played our last game together as a team. We gave everything we had, and the only reason I'm down is because we'll never experience this kind of thing again.'

"What's neat about that is that it was a kid who put it into perspective. That's one of those rare moments. It's bigger than any victory."

The sport of football could use more coaches like Mickey Heinecken.

Thursday September 18

MUSIC is well said to be the speech of angels; in fact, nothing among the utterances allowed to man is felt to be so divine. It brings us near to the infinite.

Thomas Carlyle

Friday September 19

HOCKEY teams are in training camps at this time of year. I remember the comment of Will Rogers, one of America's great humorists, on hockey.

"I saw a game here Saturday night, and war is kind of effeminate after that."

Saturday September 20

WHEN the day returns, call us up with morning faces and with morning hearts eager to labour, happy if happiness be our portion, and if the day be marked for sorrow, strong to endure.

Robert Louis Stevenson

Sunday September 21

WHOSO trusteth in the Lord, happy is he.

Proverbs 16:20

Monday September 22

WE herald the arrival of that most beautiful of the seasons, autumn. These poetic words from Edith Shaw Butler bring this beautiful time of year into focus.

This is autumn wealth untold:

Maples flaming; bronze and gold
Elms against the clear blue sky;
An orchard where ripe apples lie
Half-hidden by the uncut grass;
Crimson sumac, sassafras,
And classic oaks that overlook
Smoky asters by the brook;
Orange bittersweet, corn in shocks;
In my garden, lingering phlox.

Harvests gathered, harvests stored,
Infinite blessings of the Lord.
Why should the heart hold any less
Than a deep abiding thankfulness?

Tuesday September 23

MARG and I went to our local conservation area today, a lovely place for a fall walk. We were surprised to see a large number of school buses and cars in the parking lot. As it turned out we had happened to arrive at the district cross-country running meet. For the uninitiated this is an incredible sight.

At the high school level competitors are divided into three divisions, midget, junior and senior with boys and girls running separately.

In today's competition schools were allowed an unlimited number of runners in each division which meant that upwards of two hundred runners were running in each division.

Watching these young athletes take off together at the crack of a gun is an awe-inspiring sight. To the untrained eye it resembles an enormous stampede but according to the coach with whom I spoke each athlete has his or her own strategy for running the race.

It is interesting to note that runners are running both for themselves and for a team placing—that team with the lowest total of their top four runners' placings being the winner.

The grit and determination shown by these young athletes as they crossed the finish line brought tears to my eyes.

Wednesday September 24

LET us pray not for lighter burdens but for stronger backs.

Thursday September 25

WITH the many special discounts given to seniors who travel, more and more of us are being bitten by the travel bug.

Unfortunately the travel bug is sometimes not the only bug to bite, particularly if you have chosen to travel in some of the more exotic locales.

When visiting a country where medical facilities may be unreliable, it is wise to take along your own traveller's kit to reduce the risk of contracting diseases and infections.

There are comprehensive medical kits available containing such items as sterilized needles, syringes, suture materials and bandages. These low cost kits are available in most areas across the country and are a welcome asset in case of emergency.

To have such a kit with you, unneeded, is certainly better than not having it when the situation is desperate.

Friday September 26

AN optimist sees an opportunity in every calamity; a pessimist sees a calamity in every opportunity.

Saturday September 27

WILL and Muriel came by today pleased to show me the pictures of the newest addition to their family, a baby boy named Eric.

Will confided in me, out of Muriel's hearing, "You know, Edna, I'm as proud as can be to be a great-grandfather but I've got to say that this is about the homeliest baby I've ever seen. I would never say it to my daughter, of course, but this little guy is not very handsome yet."

I think Will's last word says it all, "yet." Who of us has not known a rather odd-looking baby who grew up to be strikingly handsome or beautiful.

As I reminded Will—he will do well to remember the story of the "Ugly Duckling."

Sunday September 28

THE eternal God is thy refuge, and underneath are the everlasting arms.

Deuteronomy 33:27

Monday September 29

IN time of trouble go not out of yourself to seek for aid; for the whole benefit of trial consists in silence, patience, rest, and resignation. In this condition divine strength is found for the hard warfare, because God Himself fights for the soul.

Tuesday September 30

Now by the brook the maple leans
With all his glory spread,
And all the sumachs on the hills
Have turned their green to red.

Wilfred Campbell

October

Wednesday October 1

A<small>N</small> ancient basket, woven of bronze reeds,
Heaped high with frosted globes of summer
    fruit:
Two crimson pomegranates with tangy seeds,
Apples and grapes, nurtured from sap and root,
An orange gold as any harvest moon:
Fruit frosted and cooled from slanting silver
    rain . . .
The highlights on it are like summer noon,
Or like the gold light on September grain.

The labour and the love of this good year,
The glowing colours flowing from God's hand,
The sun, the soil, the rain, all gathered here . . .
A miracle no heart may understand.
More beautiful than any flowers are these—
This basket holds the shining gift of trees.

Grace Noll Crowell

Thursday October 2

A DEAR friend of mine had a difficult decision to make this week. After several years of coping with her husband's Alzheimer's disease she concluded that home care was no longer possible and that a nursing home was where he needed to be.

The decision to place a loved one in a nursing home is never an easy one to make. For Frances, who just celebrated her fifty-third year of marriage to Bob, it was heartbreaking.

"It was difficult to remember the exact first signs of his illness, Edna. Looking back I know that the evidence was there years before the actual diagnosis. Simple things such as packing up his toolbox seemed to confound him. Conversations sometimes took strange and confusing turns. Because he was so clever I just assumed that his thoughts moved more quickly than mine.

"Eventually these mild symptoms became disturbing. He began reading *The Financial Post* aloud as if by hearing the words they might make more sense.

"A fastidious dresser, he began wearing bizarre clothing combinations.

"When he could no longer feed himself, and began having seizures, Edna, I knew I couldn't cope any more."

It still doesn't make it an easy decision—just a wise one.

Friday October 3

I DO not believe there is a problem in this country or the world today which could not be settled if approached through the teaching of the Sermon on the Mount.

Harry S. Truman

Saturday October 4

L ET every dawn of the morning be to you as the beginning of life. And let every setting of the sun be to you as its close. Then let everyone of these short lives leave its sure record of some kindly thing done for others; some good strength or knowledge gained for yourself.

John Ruskin

Sunday October 5

T HOU, Lord, in the beginning hast laid the foundation of the earth: and the heavens are the work of thy hand.

They shall perish but thou shalt endure. . . .

Psalm 102:25-26

Monday October 6

R AY MacMillan, a widower and good friend of our family, has a very interesting winter planned for himself. He is going to be a gentleman cruise host on one of the Cunard liners.

He has always wanted to travel but his budget is limited. This seems like the perfect answer.

A number of the Cunard ships engage anywhere from four to ten gentleman hosts per cruise to provide single female passengers with dance partners and the opportunity to socialize at the many cocktail parties and entertainment events on board ship.

These hosts are over 45, are proficient ballroom dancers, and have diversified interests and highly polished social skills.

Ray certainly meets the criteria and I know that the ladies on the cruise will enjoy the company of this outgoing and friendly gentleman.

Tuesday October 7

W IRE to a college football coach on the eve of the "Big Game":

"We're 100% behind you, coach, win or draw."

Wednesday October 8

THIS was a very busy day for our seniors group. This coming weekend is our local fall fair and we needed to put the finishing touches on a number of our entries in the baking, produce and crafts displays.

Our pride and joy this year is a quilt that each and every member of our group had a hand in producing. At first it took some convincing to get the male members of our crowd to join our efforts—some of them weren't too sure that they wanted to sew.

However, after John told us the story of the great N.H.L. goaltender, Jacques Plante, knitting his own long underwear in the Montreal Canadiens dressing room, the gentlemen seemed a little more inclined toward participation. In fact, the men seemed to have the best eye toward the colour-matching of our fabrics.

So it was with great pride that our group leader, Lorena, transported our finished quilt to the hall where it will be judged along with the many other fine productions.

Thursday October 9

ONE way to live happily ever after is not to be after too much.

Friday October 10

SMART people speak from experience. Smarter people, from experience, do not speak.

Saturday October 11

WHAT a splendid day! As well as being our Fall Fair it is our Thanksgiving weekend. This is the first time that the fair has been planned to coincide with Thanksgiving and judging from the size of the crowd today it has been a successful decision.

We went as a large family group and each of us enjoyed the fair a little differently. The children loved the "petting zoo" where they could touch the farm animals. As well they were thrilled by the rides in the midway area.

I enjoyed the crafts and the produce but I think that we all agreed that the homemade apple pie and ice cream were the hit of the fair.

Our quilt picked up a beautiful second place ribbon of which we may be proud, and our muffins took home the first place red ribbon.

Any of you looking for an enjoyable fall outing need look no further than the many fall fairs in every area of our province.

Sunday October 12

THANK you for the world so sweet,
Thank you for the food we eat,

Thank you for the birds that sing,
Thank you God for everything.

A child's prayer of thanksgiving.

Monday October 13

ON this Thanksgiving Day here in Canada we
have so much to be thankful for. We have so
many freedoms that we take for granted—free
speech, freedom of religion and worship, the freedom to choose our government and our destiny.

These are all an important part of the democ-
racy that is our heritage.

Enjoy this day and give thanks for all that we
enjoy.

Tuesday October 14

IF we are intended for great ends, we are called
to great hazards.

Henry Cardinal Newman

Wednesday October 15

BEFORE the days of television we depended on
the radio to provide us with many evenings

Perry Tanksley wrote these comforting words "What Death Is Like," and I hope they will be of some solace to the family of my friend Marcie Jones who passed away today.

I asked what death is like
And saw the eventide
Stoop down caressing earth
All sad and lone and tired.

I asked what death is like
And saw a fresh sunrise
That came expelling night
And waking sleeping eyes.

I asked what death is like
And saw a shadowed face
Of One I recognized,
A friend I should embrace.

Wednesday October 22

WE all live under the same sky, but we don't have the same horizon.

Konrad Adenauer

Thursday October 23

AFTER the first heavy frost of the year I often think of our feathered friends and the long

of entertainment. I'm sure that some of my readers can remember laughing aloud with *Fibber McGee and Molly* or listening nervously to *Lights Out*, one of the scarier presentations on the airwaves.

Who can forget the squeaking door that heralded the arrival of the *Inner Sanctum* mysteries? The show ran from 1941 to 1952 with host Raymond Edward Johnson, the only regular cast member. It featured such stars as Raymond Massey, Peter Lorre, Boris Karloff, Mary Astor and Orson Welles.

How much fun it was to close your eyes and imagine how each of the characters looked as their words echoed around the kitchen or living room on a Saturday night.

Inner Sanctum mysteries often dealt with the supernatural and took place in haunted mansions and had bizarre twists. No matter how ludicrous the story, we enjoyed listening and imagining the "terrifying" settings and characters.

Television is wonderful but I miss those old radio shows.

Thursday October 16

"MY foreman thinks I have more ability than I think I have. So I consistently do better work than I thought I could do."

From a letter in a General Motors employee contest.

Friday October 17

PEOPLE are indeed strange. Things that repel us in real life are found fascinating on a television screen.

Saturday October 18

I HATE funerals and would not attend my own if it could be avoided, but it is well for every man to stop once in a while to think of what sort of a collection of mourners he is training for his final event.

Robert T. Morris

Sunday October 19

ETERNAL God, to you, our heavenly Father, the darkness and the light are both alike and the night is as clear as day. We therefore pray you to be with those who watch and work throughout the night on behalf of others. Grant them courage in danger, diligence in emergencies, and the presence of your Holy Spirit in the long and lonely hours. When we wake may we be thankful for

their labours and take thought in turn for th needs; through Jesus Christ our Lord.

This lovely prayer came from one of the ne orders of service for the "Close of Day." It's g to see that the newer prayers have relevanc our changing world.

Monday October 20

I LIKE spring, but it is too young. I like sum but it is too proud. So I like best of all aut because its tone is mellower, its colours are ri and it is tinged with a little sorrow. Its golden ness speaks not of the innocence of spring the power of summer, but of the mellownes kindly wisdom of approaching age. It know limitations of life and is content.

Lin Y

Tuesday October 21

A PROBLEM that faces those of us who ¿ vanced in age is that our friends are no ing away at an alarming rate. For follower Christian faith, our belief in eternal life p some much needed comfort in these ti sorrow.

winter to come for them. Marg, Bruce and I always keep our feeders full of seed but when the very cold weather comes we like to provide special treats that will keep the birds returning again and again.

One of the recipes that we use very often is this:

3 parts melted fat (suet preferred)
1 part cornmeal or finely cracked corn
1 part peanut butter
1 part sunflower kernels (or chopped nuts)
1 part brown sugar
1 part chopped dried fruit (raisins, etc.)

Combine all of the ingredients with enough water to get the consistency of cooked oatmeal. Cook in a double boiler until well blended. Pour into small containers like tuna fish cans that can be securely attached to feeders or trees.

Starting early to attract birds will ensure their good health and your bird-watching pleasure.

Friday October 24

DICK McDonald, who with his brother, founded "McDonalds" the fast food chain, often told this story about his mother.

"She was Irish and to an Irish mother a steady job is very important. You could be a policeman, a garbage man, a sales clerk—as long as you brought home a steady paycheque.

"My brother and I always worked for ourselves, and this just about drove our mother crazy.

"Years went by and we became pretty successful. A friend said to her, 'I'll bet you're proud of your boys now.'

"'Well, I guess so,' Mother replied. 'But I wish they had a steady job.'"

Saturday October 25

NOTHING is lost yet, nothing broken,
And yet the cold blue word is spoken:
Say goodbye now to the Sun,
The days of love and leaves are done.

R.P.T. Coffin

Sunday October 26

BLESSED are the pure in heart, for they will see God.

Matthew 5:8

Monday October 27

ADVICE is what we ask for when we already know the answer but wish we didn't.

Erica Jong

Tuesday October 28

IF a child is to keep alive his inborn sense of wonder without any such gift from the fairies, he needs the companionship of at least one adult who can share it, rediscovering with him the joy, excitement, and mystery of the world we live in.

Rachel Carson

Wednesday October 29

MY grandson Marshall is a lawyer and he enjoyed this story that poked fun at his profession.

An elderly gentleman asked a lawyer for some legal advice. The lawyer gave the advice and as the old gentleman turned to leave said, "Excuse me. You forgot to pay me."

"What for?" asked the man.

"For my professional advice," replied the lawyer.

"I don't owe you anything—I don't intend to take it."

Thursday October 30

SOME books are to be tasted, others to be swallowed, and some few to be chewed and digested.

Francis Bacon

Friday October 31

ON this Halloween night we shall expect the little ghosts and goblins of our neighbourhood to come trick-or-treating.

Bruce and the grandchildren have carved a wonderful jack-o'-lantern and the treats are at the door ready to be given out.

Halloween is a day that I really enjoy. I have so many fond memories of making costumes for the girls. Although I could never be called a seamstress I did have a knack for putting together good imaginative costumes.

So it is with happy anticipation that I look forward to seeing our little costumed callers this evening. I know that seeing them will bring back Halloweens from long ago.

November

Saturday November 1

As soft warm days of summer change
  to autumns brilliant hues,
The early twilights linger long
  ere day and nighttime fuse
Till Indian Summer comes and goes,
  the year declines to end.
The vibrant maze of colour wanes
  and blanket leaves descend.

Across the fields in evidence
  lies harvest time o'er-spilled,
And earth rests in contentment now,
  her strivings all fulfilled.
A certain mellow peace perfects
  each golden afternoon;
Complacently, the world awaits
  the frost-white of the moon.

In autumn, then, nostalgic tears
  pour forth within my heart,
And longings welled there since the spring
  all floodingly impart—

For yearn it did for fruit to bear,
  a love to share the way—
Instead, it dwells in memory
  with dreams of yesterday. . . .

Thallis Thatcher Hoyt

Sunday November 2

O EVERLASTING Light, surpassing all created luminaries, flash forth Thy lightning from above, piercing all the most inward parts of my heart. Make clean, make glad, make bright and make alive my spirit, with all the powers thereof, that I may cleave unto Thee in ecstasies of joy.

Thomas à Kempis

Monday November 3

S OME of my closer friends are now living in retirement or nursing homes. The decision to give up one's home is not an easy one to make as these friends can attest. However, once made, it is most often met with an attitude of "Why didn't I do this long ago?"

Some of the retirement lodges are as elegant as a high quality hotel with recreation facilities second to none. Several of my friends who have lived in loneliness after their partner's death have revelled in their newfound friendships and have taken a fresh lease on life.

Those other friends who need more care than a retirement home can provide are enjoying the care and concern shown for them in nursing home facilities.

These can be some of our "golden years."

Tuesday November 4

I HAVE always enjoyed live theatre and I think that it can be a wonderful experience for children as well. My friend Mary McConnell feels as I do and some years ago she decided to take several of her ten children to a "Little Theatre" production of "I'll Be Back Before Midnight."

At that time the children's ages ranged between six and eleven years. When Mary ordered the tickets she wasn't able to get all of the seats in the same row, so she asked for three seats together and the other three seats directly behind them. The three oldest children sat in the row closer to the stage and Mary and her two youngest sat behind them.

The youngsters sat riveted to the play as it progressed. It was a "thriller" and on several occasions the two younger children clutched Mary's arms and shivered with fear. The older children assured Mary in quiet whispers that they weren't scared at all—until the gun went off.

As the murderer slunk through the open window and fired the deadly shot with an enormous BANG, three children simultaneously leaped over the back of their seats and landed right in Mary's lap.

What actor could ask for better praise?

Wednesday November 5

IF God answered everyone's prayers, the world would be filled with very old, very rich people.

R. Miller

Thursday November 6

PEOPLE often talk of the special bond between twins. I remember twin girls who were good friends of my granddaughter Phyllis. Although they were not identical they were certainly similar and the similarities were emphasized by the fact that they wore their hair cut exactly the same way. Also their taste in clothing was so close that, although they didn't wear identical outfits, their clothing had a "sameness" to it.

One of the twins moved to Vancouver to work and two years went by when the girls didn't see each other.

On the day Bev was to arrive for a visit, Les and Phyllis went to the airport to greet her. Les had cut her long blond hair very short and was anxious to surprise her twin.

As they scanned the arriving crowd, Phyllis burst out laughing. There was Beverly with the identical short hair cut and she was wearing exactly the same skirt and sweater as her twin sister.

Friday November 7

REGARDLESS of how you feel inside, always try to look like a winner. Even if you are behind, a sustained look of control and confidence can give you a mental edge that results in victory.

Arthur Ashe

Saturday November 8

A WIND has blown the rain away and blown the sky away and all the leaves away, and the trees stand. I think I too have known autumn too long.

e.e. cummings

Sunday November 9

REMEMBER, O Lord, thy tender mercies and thy lovingkindnesses for they have been ever of old.

Psalm 25:6

Monday November 10

There are good neighbours wherever you live.

Tuesday November 11

REMEMBRANCE DAY

ALTHOUGH more than fifty years have now passed since World War II ended there are those of us whose memories of those dark days remain very vivid. As one veteran said, "My work in the air force remains to this day, the most important thing that I ever did in my life. I know that the young people who haven't known war may never understand this, but it is enough that I do, and that I can look back with pride and say, "I made a difference."

Brave men who work while others sleep,
Who dare while others fly—
They build a nation's pillars deep
And lift them to the sky.

Ralph Waldo Emerson

Wednesday November 12

To gain that which is worth having, it may be necessary to lose everything else.

Bernadette Devlin

Thursday November 13

MY grandson Marshall offered this list of things he'd like to hear—but probably never will.

From his dentist: "Your teeth are so strong I won't need to see you for at least five years."

From his garage mechanic: "It was just a loose wire. No charge to fix it."

From his repair contractor: "I'm sorry. It appears that my estimate was high."

From Revenue Canada: "It seems that you've overpaid your income tax for the last few years. You can expect to receive a large cheque from us, interest included."

Friday November 14

THE ideals which have always shone before me and filled me with the joy of living are goodness, beauty, and truth.

Albert Einstein

Saturday November 15

MY great-grandson Mickey is off at university this year and his calls home have amused his parents.

When June asked if he had been separating his laundry loads he assured her that he had been putting them in three piles.

"Lights, darks and delicates?" asked June.

"No," he answered, "Dirty, really dirty, and only if we have enough money."

Sunday November 16

WHAT comforts, Lord, to those are given,
Who seek in Thee their home and rest!
They find on earth an opening heaven,
And in Thy peace are amply blest.

W.C. Dessler

Monday November 17

IT's hard for everybody to have their prayers answered while some are praying for sunshine and others for rain.

Tuesday November 18

IT has been ten years now since I first started taking piano lessons. I have not regretted a single minute of it!

All of my life I had been envious of people who could play the piano. As a child our family could not afford lessons and as an adult there didn't seem to be enough time. So rather than regret forever that I didn't at least try, I began taking lessons from a very gifted teacher with infinite patience.

I certainly can't lay claim to a great musical gift but I am able now to sit down and play with confidence and pleasure—if not with fantastic skill.

If I could offer advice to people, whatever their advanced age, it would be to go after a dream, no matter how difficult or far away it may seem.

Apparently old dogs can learn new tricks.

Wednesday November 19

IF you don't believe in cooperation, just observe what happens to a wagon when one wheel falls off.

Thursday November 20

HALF the things that people do not succeed in are through fear of making the attempt.

James Northcote

Friday November 21

WHAT is it in human nature that makes us take our loved ones for granted?

Certainly we express our love for one another on those special occasions—birthdays, anniversaries, and Christmas. Why do we seldom take a moment to express what is in our hearts without having to have a special reason?

Perhaps the saddest failure of our lives is to wait until it is too late to express our love for one another.

Saturday November 22

I CAN tell that I have enjoyed a book if I dread starting the last chapter.

Sunday November 23

O GIVE thanks unto the Lord, for He is gracious: and His mercy endureth forever.

Psalm 136:1

Monday November 24

M Y friend Jake Frampton made this interesting observation.

"If I put down a two-by-four plank on the floor everybody in the room could walk across it and not fall, because the focus would be that we would walk that two-by-four.

"If I took that same plank and put it ten stories high between two buildings few would even attempt to walk it, because the focus would be on falling.

"Much more can be accomplished if we focus on what we are doing and not on what might happen while we are doing it."

Tuesday November 25

T HE gem cannot be polished without friction.

Chinese Proverb

Wednesday November 26

I F it weren't for the last minute, a lot of things would never get done.

Thursday November 27

A HAPPY Thanksgiving to my American friends. I offer today this "untraditional" recipe for a very traditional Thanksgiving dessert, pumpkin pie.

4 ounces cream cheese, softened
1 tablespoon milk (or half-and-half)
1 tablespoon sugar
1 1/2 cups commercial whipped topping
1 ready-made Graham cracker pie crust
1 cup milk (or half-and-half)
2 packages (4-serving size) vanilla instant pudding/pie filling
1 can (16 oz.) pumpkin
1 tsp. ground cinnamon
1/2 teaspoon each ground nutmeg and allspice
1/4 teaspoon ground cloves

Mix cream cheese, milk and sugar in a large bowl. Beat until smooth. Stir in whipped topping. Spread on the bottom of the crust.

Pour 1 cup milk into bowl. Add pudding mix. Beat with wire whisk until well blended (mixture will be thick).

Stir in pumpkin and spices with wire whisk; mix well. Spread over cream cheese layer. Refrigerate at least 3 hours. Garnish with additional whipped topping if desired. Makes 8 servings.

Friday November 28

MEMORIES allow us to relive the joyful moments of our lives again and again. Many people have spoken of memory and I offer just a few of those thoughts today.

God gave us memories that we might have roses in December.

J.M. Barrie

Memory is the treasury and guardian of all things.

Cicero

A man's real possession is his memory. In nothing else is he rich, in nothing else is he poor.

Alexander Smith

THE HERITAGE BOOK

It is notorious that the memory strengthens as
you lay burdens on it and becomes trustworthy
as you trust it.

Saturday November 29

SOMETIME last night snow began to fall,
So gently did it come, so softly white;
Its music we failed to hear at all
As it whispered its song to the listening night.

The evergreens with snow are spread,
Drifts push up against the wall
Each post wears a night cap on its head,
Everything's dressed in the new snowfall.

It is pure and beautiful outside—
Within, my room is cozy and warm.
A sense of peace with me abides
As I look out at the first snowstorm.

My thanks to the unknown author.

Sunday November 30

FIRST SUNDAY IN ADVENT

OWE no man anything, but to love one another:
for he that loveth another hath fulfilled the
law.

Romans 13:8

December

Monday December 1

As we begin this last month of the year I offer Christina Rossetti's poem "The Months" which sums up our year so concisely.

January cold desolate;
February dripping wet;
March wind ranges;
April changes;
Birds sing in tune
To flowers of May,
And sunny June
Brings longest day;
In scorched July
The storm clouds fly,
Lightning torn;
August bears corn,
September fruit;
In rough October
Earth must disrobe her;
Stars fall and shoot
In keen November;
And night is long

And cold is strong
In bleak December.

Tuesday December 2

B LESSED is the servant who loves his brother
as much when he is sick and useless as when
he is well and can be of service to him. And
blessed is he who loves his brother as well when
he is afar off as when he is by his side, and who
would say nothing behind his back he might not,
in love, say before his face.

St. Francis of Assisi

Wednesday December 3

I SPENT some time working today on my
Christmas cards and on the letters that I like
to include in each one. This is one of the
Christmas "chores" that I enjoy the most. Sharing
stories of our family and of the happenings of the
year past reminds me again and again just how
lucky I am.

In turn, I am anxious to receive news from my
friends and their families, as their cards and letters
arrive.

When talking regularly with far-off friends and
relatives is not a practical possibility, the Christmas
letter is a wonderful alternative.

Thursday December 4

MARG and I spent a good portion of the day at our local nursing home helping to put up the Christmas decorations. What a wonderful time we had!

Our town newspaper had asked for donations of decorations to be dropped off at the home during the month of November. The response to this request was overwhelming!

Strings of tiny coloured lights, boxes and boxes of coloured balls, tinsel, exquisite ornaments and pine trees, both real and artificial, arrived in abundance. As well, the florists and greenhouse owners brought poinsettia plants by the dozen.

Our volunteer group arrived early this morning and with much organization and hard work managed to complete the task of decorating each resident's room as well as the many lounges, dining areas and nursing stations.

By the time we finished it was a veritable Christmas wonderland.

The best part of the day, however, came in the hour before dinner as the nurses and volunteers took each resident on a grand tour of the home. The surprise and delight on every face was a joy to see—and really, isn't this sharing of love what Christmas is all about?

Friday December 5

LIVING on a small fixed income, as so many of us seniors are, makes Christmas gift-giving a creative challenge.

Using an idea that I picked up in a magazine, I have made something special for each family member that I hope they will enjoy.

Utilizing the many boxes of photos taken over the past years I have assembled a collage of photographs of each person in our immediate family.

I began with their baby pictures and included pictures from childhood through high school, a wedding photo and so on up to the present day.

Using some coloured cardboard, I placed the trimmed pictures in chronological order. Then with a calligraphy pen I put their names and birth dates in the corner.

I found inexpensive frames (available in most local department stores) and completed each collage.

I hope that my family will enjoy seeing how they have grown and changed over the years.

It isn't always necessary to spend a lot of money on a gift. A little ingenuity can go a long way.

Saturday December 6

WE make a living by what we get; we make a life by what we give.

Sunday December 7

ON this second Sunday in Advent, our pastor reminded us of the Old Testament prophesies of the coming of the Messiah. The hymn for the day came from 15th-century France.

O come, O come, Emmanuel,
And ransom captive Israel,
That mourns in lonely exile here
Until the Son of God appear.
Rejoice! Rejoice! Emmanuel
Shall come to thee, O Israel.

Monday December 8

As the weather turns colder, ice will be forming on the Rideau Canal in our capital city of Ottawa. The canal will then become the longest skating rink in the world with close to nine kilometres of well-kept ice.

With its 47 locks and 30 control dams it has been hailed as one of the greatest engineering feats of the last century.

When the canal freezes, thousands of skaters will use it as a route to and from the office.

While some of us dread the coming of winter and the cold weather there are canal skaters in Ottawa who can hardly wait to use this unique frozen waterway.

Tuesday December 9

Hanukkah, the "Festival of Lights," is celebrated each year about this time. It celebrates the return of the Jerusalem Temple to the worship of God from Greek Syrian paganism in the year 165 B.C.

This festival is widely celebrated in Jewish homes around the world. The message of Hanukkah is that every human being—in every part of the world—must be free to worship in the way that they choose.

I pray that this message may be fulfilled worldwide.

Wednesday December 10

At this very busy time of year it is so important that we not forget our friends or family members who are shut-ins.

This can be a very lonely time for those who are unable to be out and around. A visit, no matter how brief, can mean so much.

This is a time for giving and what could be more important than giving of your time?

Thursday December 11

To our grandchildren, what we tell them about their parents' childhood and our own young years is living history.

Ruth Good

Friday December 12

THERE will come a time when you believe everything is finished. That will be the beginning.

Louis L'Amour

Saturday December 13

DON'T be afraid of showing affection. Be warm and tender, thoughtful and affectionate. Men are more helped by sympathy than by service. Love is more than money, and a kind word will give more pleasure than a present.

Sir John Lubbock

Sunday December 14

THE advent of our God
With eager prayers we greet,
And singing haste upon his road
His coming reign to meet.

The everlasting Son
Came down to make us free;
And He a servant's form put on
To gain our liberty.

Charles Coffin
(from the hymn book)

Monday December 15

Each year at this time, our local high school students have a food drive to collect for needy families in our area.

Several young people came to our door this evening to ask for contributions of non-perishable goods or clothing. Marg and I had knit several pairs of mittens and saved some tinned meats and vegetables which we were pleased to donate.

The teenagers thanked us profusely and wished us a happy Christmas season.

We hear so often of young adults who are troublemakers. I wish that more could be said of the kind and generous students who spend hours at this busy time of year trying to provide for those less fortunate than themselves.

Tuesday December 16

You are as young as your faith, as old as your doubt; as young as your self confidence, as old as your fear; as young as your hope, as old as your despair.

Samuel Ullman

Wednesday December 17

I BELIEVE that I have told this story before but I think that it is interesting enough to be repeated.

In the year 1870, the Methodists in Indiana held a conference.

The presiding bishop asked the president of the college where they were meeting to say a few words.

The president said, "We are in a very exciting age. I believe we will see wonderful inventions. I believe men will fly through the air like birds."

The bishop was offended. "I read in my Bible that flight is reserved for the angels. What you say is heretical and blasphemous."

The bishop, whose name was Wright, then went home to his two sons, Orville and Wilbur.

Thursday December 18

T HERE are moments when whatever be the attitude of the body, the soul is on its knees.

Friday December 19

PEOPLE say that Christmas today is too com-
mercialized. But I have never found it that
way. If you spend money to give people joy, you
are not being commercial. It is only when you feel
obliged to do something about Christmas that the
spirit is spoiled.

Eleanor Roosevelt

Saturday December 20

THE intelligent man finds almost everything
ridiculous, the sensible man hardly anything.

Goethe

Sunday December 21

WHILE shepherds watched their flocks by night,

All seated on the ground,
The angel of the Lord came down,
And glory shone around.

Nahum late

Monday December 22

Last evening was the presentation of the children's Christmas pageant in our church. Each year the Sunday school teachers join their classes together to present the story of the birth of Christ, and each presentation has its own special moments. Last night's was no exception.

Every child in the Sunday school class has a role in the pageant. Because of the large numbers enrolled it often means that the stable where Jesus is born is very crowded with "cows," "donkeys" and "lambs" of varying sizes and ages.

All was as practised until the "Three Wise Men" arrived bearing their "gifts." The "gold" and the "frankincense" were presented without problem but the bearer of the "myrrh" announced, "You know, Jesus is a baby. I'm sure he doesn't want this myrrh stuff so I brought him a bottle of apple juice." He then brought out a baby's bottle with nipple and filled with juice to present to the baby Jesus.

As he presented the bottle he began singing, "Happy birthday to you." To the delight of the audience he was quickly joined by every "shepherd," "cow," "donkey," "lamb" and even "Mary" and "Joseph." As they say in show business—"It brought the house down!"

Tuesday December 23

I KNOW not what the future holds, but I know who holds the future.

Wednesday December 24

I T is Christmas Eve and here in our home where many of our family have gathered together it is the quiet of the night. I am reminded of that beloved poem—

'Twas the night before Christmas
And all through the house
Not a creature was stirring
Not even a mouse . . . .

I look forward to the celebration to come.

Thursday December 25

D O not be afraid; for behold, I bring you good news of a great joy which shall be for all the people; for today in the city of David there has been born for you a Saviour, who is Christ the Lord.

Luke 2:10–11

A very Merry Christmas to you all.

Friday December 26

How nice it is to have Boxing Day as a "recovery" day after a wonderful but tiring Christmas.

As a "turkey leftover lover" I look forward to several days of turkey in many variations. Hot or cold sandwiches, pot pie, soup, cutlets are just a few of the ways to use the leftover bird.

When I was a child our family always ate a Christmas goose. I don't remember exactly when we switched to the turkey as our traditional meal but I can tell you that a turkey sandwich is infinitely nicer than a goose meat sandwich.

As Marshall remarked this morning, "I like turkey so much it would be nice to have it in a breakfast cereal flavour."

My goodness, I'd never thought of that . . . .

Saturday December 27

THE courage to imagine the otherwise is our greatest resource, adding colour and suspense to all our life.

D.J. Boorstin

Sunday December 28

> HARK! the herald angels sing,
> "Glory to the new-born King;
> Peace on earth, and mercy mild,
> God and sinners reconciled!"
> Joyful, all ye nations, rise,
> Join the triumph of the skies;
> With th'angelic hosts proclaim,
> "Christ is born in Bethlehem!"
> Hark! the herald angels sing,
> "Glory to the new-born King."

Monday December 29

ONE of the most thoughtful gifts that I received for Christmas was a large supply of long distance gift certificates for the telephone.

As we get older, I know that thinking of appropriate gifts for us is difficult. What better way is there to help make our lives more enjoyable than to enable us to talk with distant friends and relatives? I hope that this gift will become an annual one.

Tuesday December 30

Your religion is not what you profess to believe; it's the way you live.

John Luther

Wednesday December 31

I WOULD like to end the year with an old Irish blessing.

May the blessing of light be on you, light without and light within.

May the blessed sunlight shine upon you and warm your heart till it glows like a great peat fire, so that the stranger may come and warm himself at it, and also a friend.

And may the light shine out of the eyes of you, like a candle set in the windows of a house, bidding the wanderer to come in out of the storm.

And may the blessing of the rain be on you—the soft sweet rain. May it fall upon your spirit so that all the little flowers may spring up, and shed their sweetness on the air.

And may the blessing of the great rains be on you, may they beat upon your spirit and wash it fair and clean, and leave there many a shining pool where the blue of heaven shines, and sometimes a star.

And may the blessing of the earth be on you— the great round earth; may you ever have a kindly greeting for them you pass as you're going along the roads. May the earth be soft under you when you rest upon it, tired at the end of a day, and may it rest easy over you when, at the last, you lie under it.

May it rest so lightly over you that your soul may be off from under it quickly, and up and off, and on its way to God.

And now may the Lord bless you and bless you kindly.